This book belongs to:

LEISURE ARTS, INC.
Little Rock, Arkansas

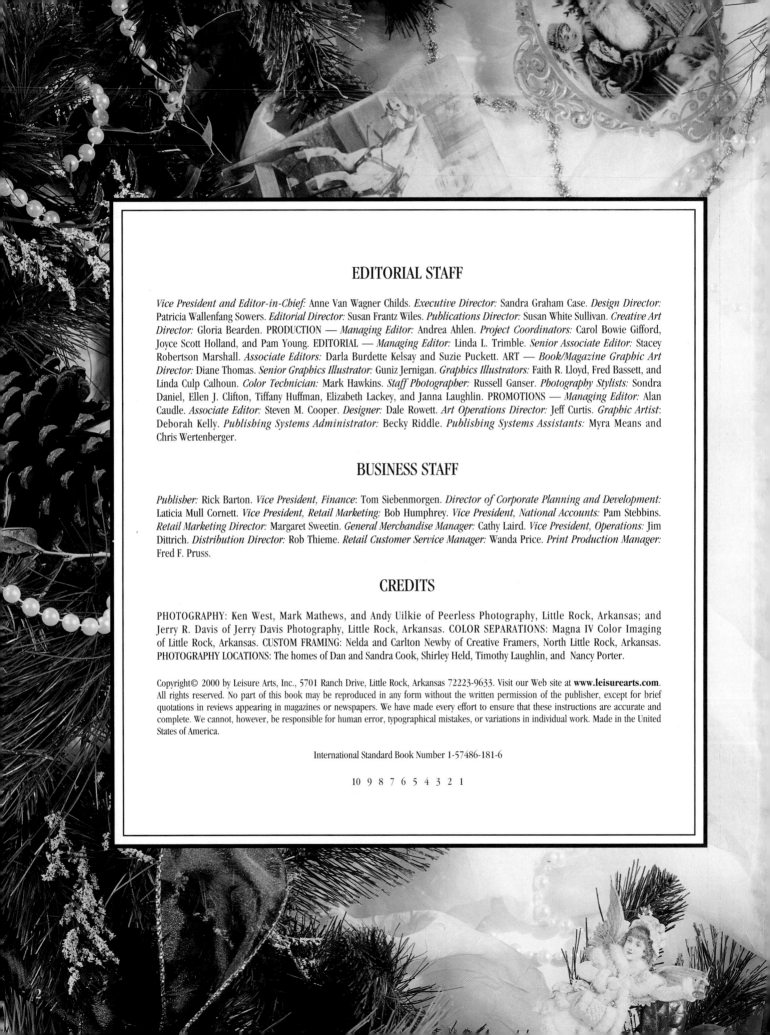

EDITORIAL STAFF

Vice President and Editor-in-Chief: Anne Van Wagner Childs. *Executive Director:* Sandra Graham Case. *Design Director:* Patricia Wallenfang Sowers. *Editorial Director:* Susan Frantz Wiles. *Publications Director:* Susan White Sullivan. *Creative Art Director:* Gloria Bearden. PRODUCTION — *Managing Editor:* Andrea Ahlen. *Project Coordinators:* Carol Bowie Gifford, Joyce Scott Holland, and Pam Young. EDITORIAL — *Managing Editor:* Linda L. Trimble. *Senior Associate Editor:* Stacey Robertson Marshall. *Associate Editors:* Darla Burdette Kelsay and Suzie Puckett. ART — *Book/Magazine Graphic Art Director:* Diane Thomas. *Senior Graphics Illustrator:* Guniz Jernigan. *Graphics Illustrators:* Faith R. Lloyd, Fred Bassett, and Linda Culp Calhoun. *Color Technician:* Mark Hawkins. *Staff Photographer:* Russell Ganser. *Photography Stylists:* Sondra Daniel, Ellen J. Clifton, Tiffany Huffman, Elizabeth Lackey, and Janna Laughlin. PROMOTIONS — *Managing Editor:* Alan Caudle. *Associate Editor:* Steven M. Cooper. *Designer:* Dale Rowett. *Art Operations Director:* Jeff Curtis. *Graphic Artist:* Deborah Kelly. *Publishing Systems Administrator:* Becky Riddle. *Publishing Systems Assistants:* Myra Means and Chris Wertenberger.

BUSINESS STAFF

Publisher: Rick Barton. *Vice President, Finance:* Tom Siebenmorgen. *Director of Corporate Planning and Development:* Laticia Mull Cornett. *Vice President, Retail Marketing:* Bob Humphrey. *Vice President, National Accounts:* Pam Stebbins. *Retail Marketing Director:* Margaret Sweetin. *General Merchandise Manager:* Cathy Laird. *Vice President, Operations:* Jim Dittrich. *Distribution Director:* Rob Thieme. *Retail Customer Service Manager:* Wanda Price. *Print Production Manager:* Fred F. Pruss.

CREDITS

PHOTOGRAPHY: Ken West, Mark Mathews, and Andy Uilkie of Peerless Photography, Little Rock, Arkansas; and Jerry R. Davis of Jerry Davis Photography, Little Rock, Arkansas. COLOR SEPARATIONS: Magna IV Color Imaging of Little Rock, Arkansas. CUSTOM FRAMING: Nelda and Carlton Newby of Creative Framers, North Little Rock, Arkansas. PHOTOGRAPHY LOCATIONS: The homes of Dan and Sandra Cook, Shirley Held, Timothy Laughlin, and Nancy Porter.

International Standard Book Number 1-57486-181-6

10 9 8 7 6 5 4 3 2 1

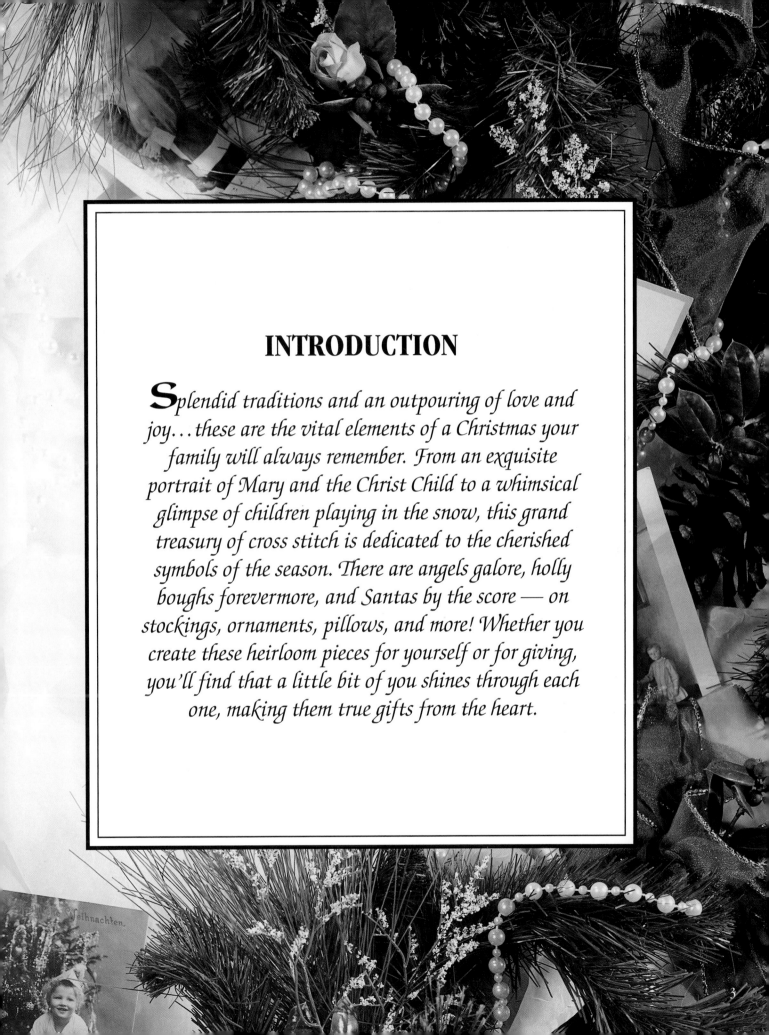

INTRODUCTION

Splendid traditions and an outpouring of love and joy…these are the vital elements of a Christmas your family will always remember. From an exquisite portrait of Mary and the Christ Child to a whimsical glimpse of children playing in the snow, this grand treasury of cross stitch is dedicated to the cherished symbols of the season. There are angels galore, holly boughs forevermore, and Santas by the score — on stockings, ornaments, pillows, and more! Whether you create these heirloom pieces for yourself or for giving, you'll find that a little bit of you shines through each one, making them true gifts from the heart.

TABLE OF CONTENTS

SILENT NIGHT

On a star-filled night long, long ago,
God bestowed upon the Virgin Mary
and mankind a most precious gift.
The birth of the Christ Child gave the
world a Saviour and brought exuberant
celebration throughout the land. During
this special season, remember the blessed
event with a beautifully stitched piece,
or display the radiant mother and
child on a door or evergreen.

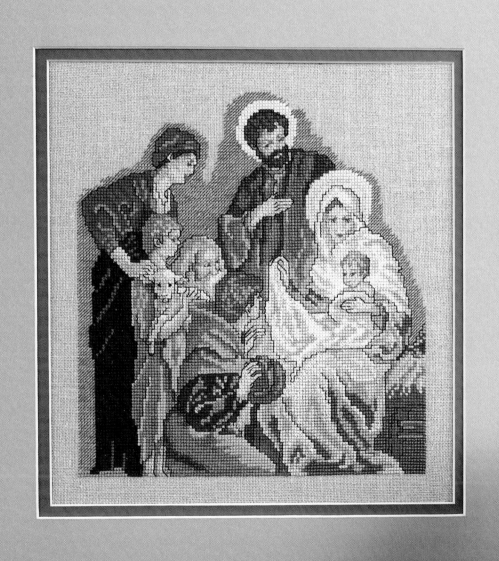

Chart on pages 42-45

SANTA'S STEED

his pack overflowing with gifts for one
and all, old St. Nick takes pause to enjoy a
last-minute ride on his magnificent horse
— a most impressive sample of elfin
handiwork! It won't be long before Santa
begins his all-night journey onward and
upward, dropping down chimneys to
surprise boys and girls with wonderful
toys. You'll enjoy displaying this
handsome piece in your holiday
home or delivering a special
gift in a handsome bag.

Chart on pages 46-49

9

PRETTY PILLOWS

As soft and pristine as the wings of angels, these snow-white pillows will add a delicate touch to your home. Trimmed with lace, pearly beads, and exquisite stitching, our heavenly cushions also make wonderful heirlooms to pass on to friends and family. Dangle one from a door knob, or toss a grouping onto a sofa or chair — such an enchanting way to share the innocence of the Christmas season with others.

Charts on pages 50-52

11

TIDINGS FROM ABOVE

A breathtaking vision with delicate wings and a flowing robe, an angel of God descends upon a quietly slumbering Bethlehem. She heralds the arrival of the Newborn King, whose birth brought hope to believers around the world. Add the beauty of this heavenly messenger to your tree or mantel and enjoy the warmth of peace and goodwill she brings to your home.

ELIZABETH

Chart on pages 62-66

GRANDFATHER FROST

Not even the whirling snow will stop Grandfather Frost from making his Yuletide trek to deliver treasures to good little boys and girls. His impressive evergreen, all aglow with candlelight, makes a beautiful addition to a holiday sweater or handsome portrait.

Charts on pages 53-55

15

WOODLAND CELEBRATION

Deep in the dense and snowy woodland, creatures great and small gather to share a bit of holiday spirit with Father Winter. He sits atop a throne fit for royalty — just right for the king of gift-giving! Our beribboned sampler and elegant tasseled ornaments will bring the beauty of nature into your home.

Chart on pages 56-59

Chart on pages 56-59

Chart on pages 58-59

ᵇave your own woodland
celebration as you cuddle up with our
cozy afghan. Add extra warmth with a
decorative band that transforms a simple
candle into a lovely accent piece.

19

NOSTALGIC TOUCHES

Create the nostalgic look of days gone by throughout your home with this pretty collection of stitched pieces. Display a treasured holiday picture in our intricate beaded frame, or sprinkle your tree with frame ornaments surrounding your favorite photos or postcards. Ball ornaments featuring traditional Christmas motifs look extra special dressed with gold trim and tassels.

Charts on pages 60-61

CHRISTMAS BLESSINGS

*T*he holiday season is a perfect time
for reflecting on the past and giving
thanks for our abundant blessings. Just
as they did on the night of a very special
birth, graceful seraphs share the news of
God's precious gift on this glorious framed
piece and fancy fringed afghan. May these
exquisite angels bring good tidings to your
home, family, and friends for many
Christmases to come.

Chart on pages 76-79

*L*et your heavenly celebration spread from room to room with a sprinkling of handmade treasures — a petite pillow, celestial tree ornaments, or an inspired bellpull.

Chart on page 76

Chart on pages 76-77 and 79

Chart on pages 76-79

YULETIDE TOYS

Dolls, teddy bears, drums, and trains
— Santa's elves have been busy all year
long making treasures to fill his
magnificent pack! Children will wait with
unbridled anticipation for the sound of
tiny hooves on the roof, announcing the
arrival of the famous gift-giver. Our
charming tree ornaments and handsome
personalized stocking will capture this
childhood moment and bring holiday
joy to the truly young at heart.

Charts on pages 67-71 and 94

MERRY GENTLEMEN

Whether wearing a flowing cloak or the familiar crimson suit, Santa Claus has been an integral part of our Christmas celebrations for centuries. Featuring some of the many images of the generous elf, our enchanted ornaments, trimmed with golden charms, will give your tree or garland an Olde World feel.

Charts on pages 72-73

SEASON'S GREETINGS

$\mathcal{D}$uring the Yuletide, goodwill seems to be everywhere — friends, family, even strangers on the street all have merry season's greetings to share. Well-wishers who come calling at your home will feel warmly welcomed by our elegant beaded ornament and striking framed piece. Both are beautiful expressions of good tidings.

Charts on pages 74-75

GLORIOUS SAMPLING

In days of old, the Yuletide was welcomed with the glow of candlelight and the scent of freshly cut evergreens. Our charming sampler collection is reminiscent of these simpler times. Cross stitched with love, the tasseled ornament, homespun pillow, and personalized stocking will add a bit of nostalgia to your holiday decorating or gift-giving.

Charts on pages 86-87

33

Ready to fill with treasures, our sampler stocking shares the glorious story of Christ's humble birth in a manger.

34

Chart on pages 84-85

CHRISTMAS IS FOR CHILDREN

Oh what joy it is to see the sparkle of excitement in the eyes of little ones at Christmastime. They marvel at the twinkling lights and colorful decorations, wait eagerly for a visit from Santa Claus, and shout with glee as they run and play in the snow. With so many fascinating things to enjoy, no wonder people say that Christmas is for children. In pretty Victorian style, our sweet pillow and holly-trimmed bellpull pay tribute to the childhood pleasures of the Yuletide season.

Christmas is for

Sharing

Laughing

the Caring Gifford Family

FROSTY
FUN

With his eyes of coal and handsome top hat, this kindly gent made of snow has charms no one can resist! Friendly children are magically drawn to the frosty fellow on our whimsical stitched piece, and crisp snowflakes add wintry flair to a muffler and gloves. What heartwarming visions!

Charts on pages 81-83

TINY
TREASURES

Some of life's very best gifts come
in small packages, and these tiny treasures
are no exception. Roses, buttons, and
ribbon bows will add a little romance
to your Christmas giving or decorating.
Tug at the heartstrings of a special friend
with a diminutive purse ornament or a
heart-embellished needle roll. Display
delicate stitched pieces in our unique
button frame or golden box to
make touching tokens of your love.

Charts on pages 92-93

SILENT NIGHT

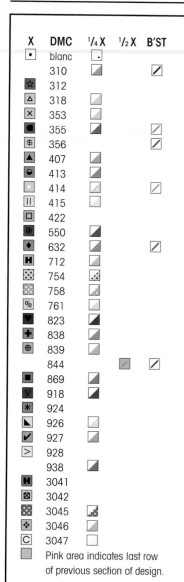

X	DMC	¼X	½X	B'ST
•	blanc	•		
	310	◣		╱
☆	312			
△	318	◣		
✕	353	◣		
◼	355	◣		╱
$	356			╱
▲	407	◣		
◉	413	◣		
▢	414	◣		╱
‖	415	◣		
▫	422			
◉	550	◣		
◆	632	◣		╱
H	712	◣		
▨	754	◢		
▨	758	◢		
%	761	◣		
▼	823	◣		
✚	838	◣		
⊕	839	◣		
	844	▨		╱
◼	869	◣		
◩	918	◣		
✳	924			
◤	926	◣		
✔	927	◣		
▷	928			
	938	◣		
H	3041			
⊠	3042			
▨	3045	◢		
❖	3046	◣		
C	3047	▫		

Pink area indicates last row of previous section of design.

Silent Night in Frame (shown on page 7): The design was stitched over 2 fabric threads on a 16" square of Zweigart ® Raw Belfast Linen (32 ct). Two strands of floss were used for Cross Stitch and 1 strand for Half Cross Stitch and Backstitch. It was custom framed.

Design by Carol Emmer.

Continued on page 44.

STITCH COUNT (120w x 127h)

14 count	8⅝"	x	9⅛"
16 count	7½"	x	8"
18 count	6¾"	x	7⅛"
22 count	5½"	x	5⅞"

SILENT NIGHT

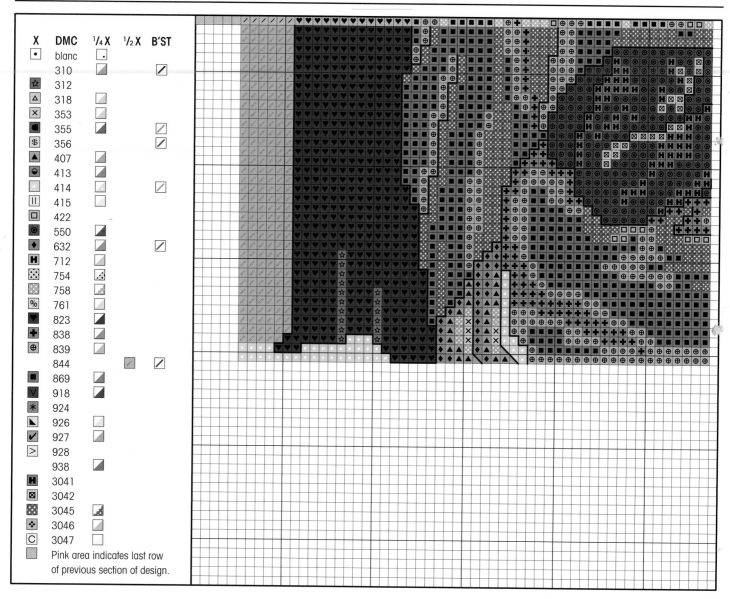

X	DMC	¼ X	½ X	B'ST
•	blanc	•		
	310	◢		◢
☆	312			
△	318	◢		
✕	353	◢		
◼	355	◢		◢
$	356			◢
▲	407	◢		
◐	413	◢		
▨	414	◢		◢
‖	415	◢		
▢	422			
◉	550	◢		
◆	632	◢		◢
H	712	◢		
▨	754	◢		
▨	758	◢		
%	761	◢		
▼	823	◢		
✚	838	◢		
⊕	839	◢		
	844	◢		◢
◼	869	◢		
◥	918	◢		
✳	924			
✔	926	◢		
>	927			
	928			
	938	◢		
H	3041			
⊠	3042			
▨	3045	◢		
✤	3046	◢		
C	3047	◢		

Pink area indicates last row of previous section of design.

Mary and Christ Child Ornament (shown on page 6): A portion of the design (refer to photo) was stitched over 2 fabric threads on a 10" x 11" piece of Zweigart® Raw Belfast Linen (32 ct). Two strands of floss were used for Cross Stitch and 1 strand for Backstitch.

For ornament, you will need a 6" x 7" piece of Raw Belfast Linen for backing, five 4 yd lengths each of DMC 924 and DMC 926 floss for twisted cord and hanger, 2½" tassel, and polyester fiberfill.

Centering design, trim stitched piece to measure 6" x 7". Matching right sides and raw edges, pin stitched piece and backing fabric together. Leaving an opening for turning, use a ½" seam allowance to sew ornament front and backing fabric together. Trim seam allowances diagonally at corners; turn ornament right side out, carefully pushing corners outward.

Stuff ornament with polyester fiberfill and blind stitch opening closed.

For twisted cord, place lengths of floss together and fold in half; tie a knot 2" from each end. Place the loop over a stationary object; pulling floss until taut, twist floss in a clockwise motion until tight. Holding floss at center to keep taut, fold floss in half matching knotted ends (**Fig.1**). Release floss at fold; floss will twist together. Secure knotted ends by tying an overhand knot. Pull cord through fingers to evenly distribute twists. Beginning and ending at bottom center of ornament, blind stitch cord around edges of ornament.

For hanger, fold a 9" length of cord in half. Referring to photo, tack hanger to top of ornament and tassel to bottom of ornament.

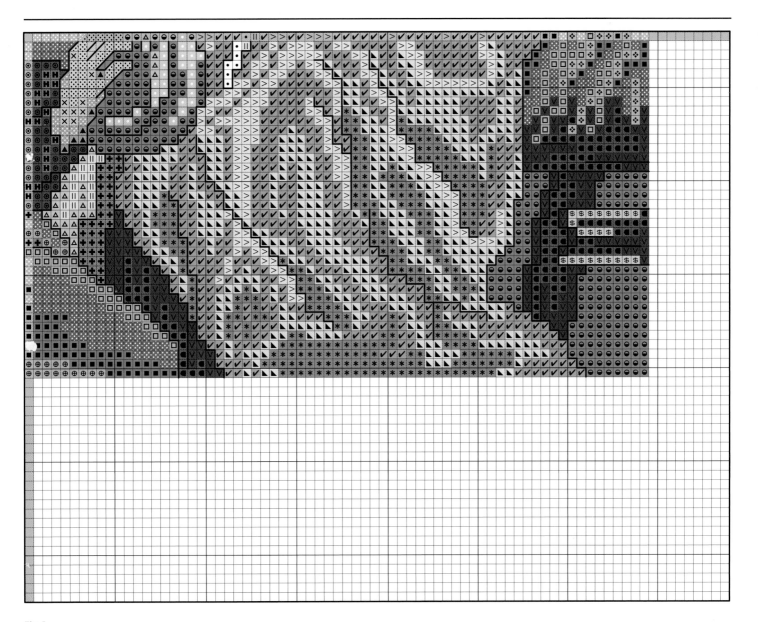

Fig. 1

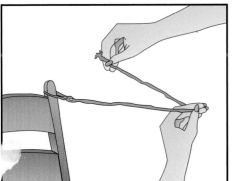

SANTA'S STEED

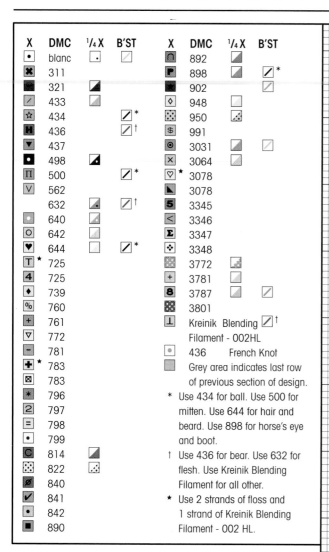

X	DMC	¼ X	B'ST	X	DMC	¼ X	B'ST
•	blanc	•	◹	∩	892		◹
✖	311			ℙ	898		◹ *
■	321	◣		✖	902		◹
╱	433	◹		◇	948		
☆	434		◹ *	⁂	950	⬚	
H	436		◹ †	$	991		
▼	437			◉	3031		◹
◨	498	◣		X	3064		◹
Π	500		◹ *	♡ *	3078		
V	562			◣	3078		
	632	◤	◹ †	5	3345		
	640	◹		<	3346		
O	642	◹		Σ	3347		
♥	644		◹ *	❖	3348		
T *	725			▦	3772	◹	
4	725			+	3781		
♦	739			8	3787		◹
%	760			▓	3801		
+	761			⊥	Kreinik Blending		◹ †
▽	772				Filament - 002HL		
–	781			●	436	French Knot	
✚ *	783				Grey area indicates last row		
⊠	783				of previous section of design.		
✳	796						
2	797						
=	798			*	Use 434 for ball. Use 500 for		
•	799				mitten. Use 644 for hair and		
C	814	◹			beard. Use 898 for horse's eye		
▨	822	⬚			and boot.		
Ø	840			†	Use 436 for bear. Use 632 for		
✔	841				flesh. Use Kreinik Blending		
•	842				Filament for all other.		
■	890			✦	Use 2 strands of floss and		
					1 strand of Kreinik Blending		
					Filament - 002 HL.		

Santa's Steed in Frame (shown on page 9): The design was stitched on a 20" x 26" piece of Zweigart® Black Aida (14 ct). Three strands of floss were used for Cross Stitch and 1 strand for Backstitch and French Knots. It was custom framed.

Santa's Gift Bag (shown on page 8): A portion of the design (refer to photo) was stitched on a 17" x 19" piece of Zweigart® Black Aida (18 ct). Three strands of floss were used for Cross Stitch and 1 strand for Backstitch and French Knots.

For bag, you will need two 23" x 36" pieces of fabric, tracing paper, fabric marking pencil, a 42" length of ³/₈"w flat braid, a 54" length of ¹/₄" dia. cord, and clear-drying craft glue.

For stitched piece pattern, fold tracing paper in fourths and place folds on dashed lines of Gift Bag Pattern, page 81; trace pattern onto tracing paper. Cut out pattern; unfold and press flat.

Referring to photo, position pattern on wrong side of stitched piece; pin pattern in place. Use a fabric marking pencil to draw around pattern; remove pattern and cut out on drawn line.

For front of bag, center stitched piece horizontally on one fabric piece with bottom of stitched piece 5¹/₂" from one short edge of fabric; pin in place. Attach stitched piece to fabric using a zigzag stitch. Beginning and ending at bottom center, glue braid around stitched piece, covering raw edges.

Continued on page 48.

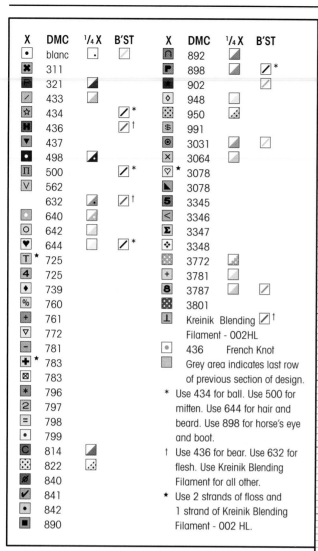

X	DMC	¼X	B'ST	X	DMC	¼X	B'ST
•	blanc	•	◲	∩	892		◲
✖	311			▛	898	◲	◿*
▛	321	◼		★	902		◲
⟋	433	◲		◇	948		◱
☆	434		◿*	▦	950	▨	
▥	436		◿†	$	991		
▼	437			◉	3031	◲	◲
◼	498	◢		✕	3064	◲	
Π	500		◿*	♡*	3078	◲	
V	562			◣	3078		
	632	◢	◿†	5	3345		
▣	640	◲		<	3346		
◎	642	◲		Σ	3347		
♥	644	◱	◿*	❖	3348		
T*	725			▦	3772	◢	
4	725			+	3781		◲
◆	739			8	3787		◲
%	760			▨	3801		
+	761			⊥	Kreinik Blending		◿†
▽	772				Filament - 002HL		
−	781			⊙	436 French Knot		
✚*	783			▨	Grey area indicates last row		
⊠	783				of previous section of design.		
✳	796						
2	797						
=	798						
•	799						
◖	814	◢					
▨	822	▨					
Ø	840						
✔	841						
•	842						
◼	890						

* Use 434 for ball. Use 500 for mitten. Use 644 for hair and beard. Use 898 for horse's eye and boot.

† Use 436 for bear. Use 632 for flesh. Use Kreinik Blending Filament for all other.

* Use 2 strands of floss and 1 strand of Kreinik Blending Filament - 002 HL.

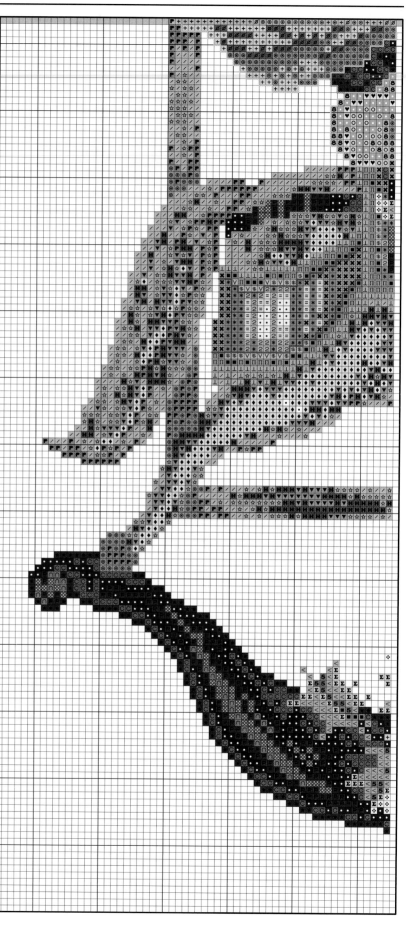

Matching right sides and leaving top edge open, use a ½" seam allowance to sew bag front and back together. For boxed corners, match each side seam to bottom seam; sew across each corner 1" from point (**Fig. 1**).

Fig. 1

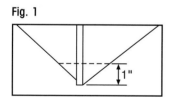

Press top edge of pack ½" to wrong side; turn ¾" to wrong side again and hem. Turn bag right side out.

Tie an overhand knot at ends of cord; tie cord around top of bag.

Design by Donna Vermillion Giampa.

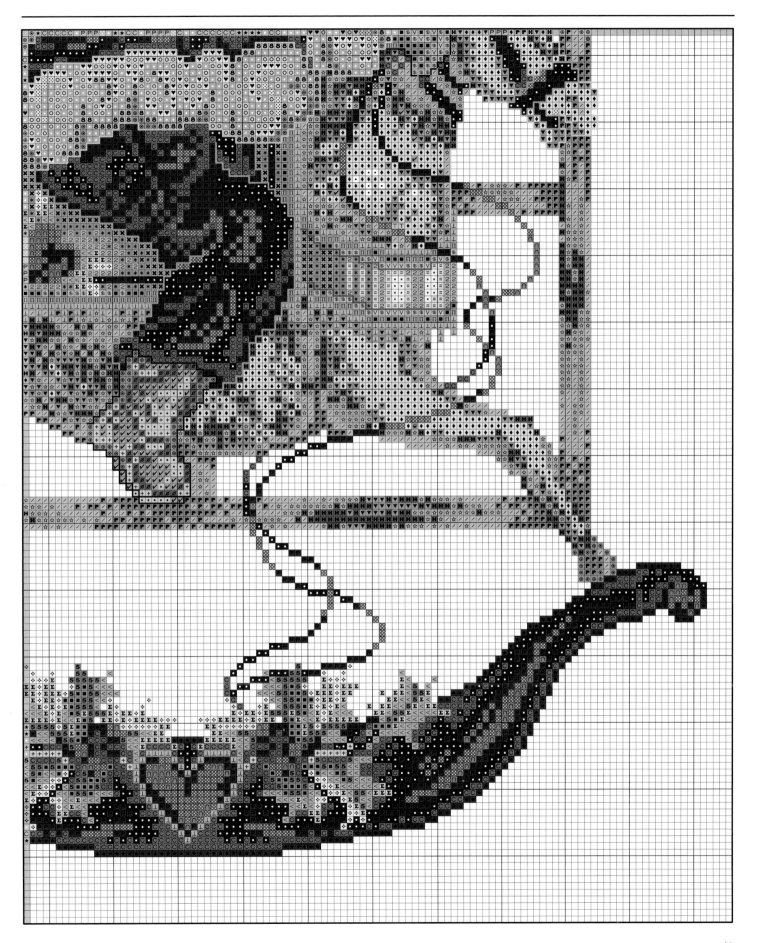

PRETTY PILLOWS

Mill Hill Bead - 03021

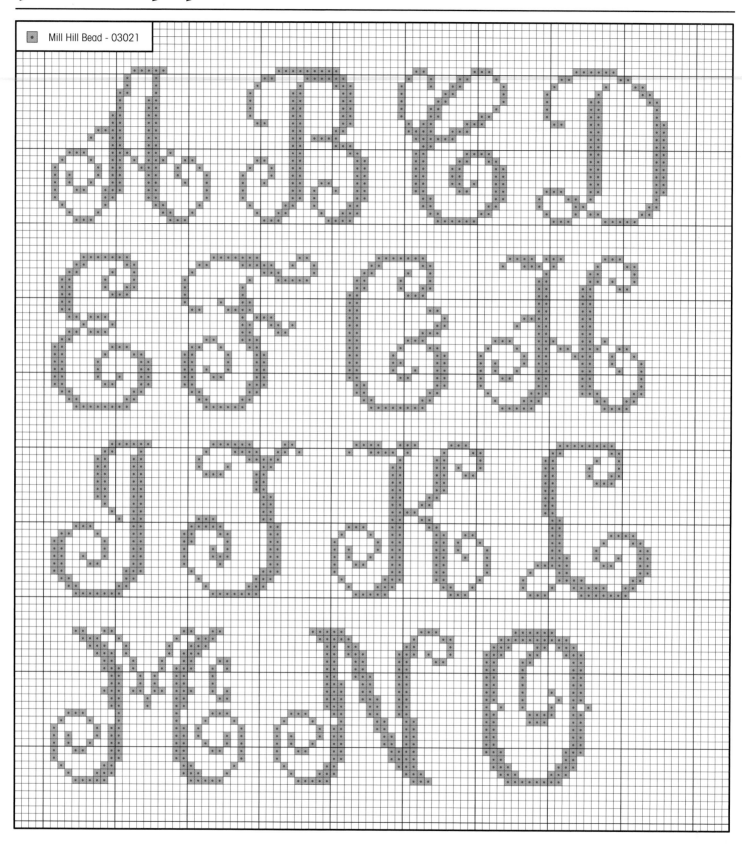

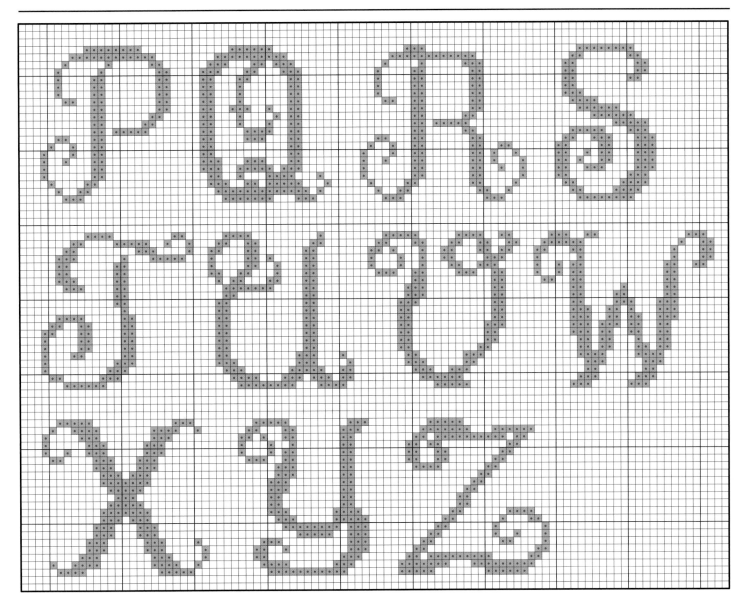

Monogram Pillow (shown on page 11): The letter "D" was worked over 2 fabric threads on a 12" square of Zweigart® Cream Cashel Linen® (28 ct). Attach beads using 1 strand of DMC ecru floss. Referring to photo, work a single row of beads 2" from letter on all sides; randomly attach beads around letter as desired. See Attaching Beads, page 95.

For pillow, you will need a 9" square of fabric for backing and polyester fiberfill.

Centering design, trim stitched piece to measure 9" square.

Matching right sides and leaving an opening for turning, use a 1/2" seam allowance to sew stitched piece and backing fabric together. Trim seam allowances diagonally at corners; turn pillow right side out, carefully pushing corners outward. Stuff pillow with polyester fiberfill and blind stitch opening closed.

Monogram Sachet Pillow (shown on page 10): The letter "H" was worked over 2 fabric threads on a 6" square of Zweigart® Cream Belfast Linen (32 ct). Attach beads using 1 strand of DMC ecru floss. See Attaching Beads, page 95.

For sachet, you will need a 4 1/2" x 4" piece of Cream Belfast Linen for backing, assorted pearl beads for fringe, 7" length of 1/4"w ribbon for hanger, and polyester fiberfill.

Centering design, trim stitched piece to measure 4 1/2" x 4".

Matching right sides and leaving an opening for turning, use a 1/2" seam allowance to sew stitched piece and backing fabric together. Trim seam allowances diagonally at corners; turn sachet pillow right side out, carefully pushing corners outward. Stuff sachet pillow with polyester fiberfill and blind stitch opening closed.

For pearl fringe, refer to photo and use 1 strand of DMC ecru floss to string assorted pearl beads. Attach pearl fringe to bottom edge of sachet pillow.

For hanger, refer to photo and tack ribbon to top corners of sachet pillow.

Pearl Pillow (shown on page 11): For pillow, you will need 5mm pearl beads, two 11" squares of fabric for pillow front and back, 44" length of 1/4" dia. purchased cording with attached seam allowance, and polyester fiberfill.

For pillow front, refer to photo and randomly attach pearl beads to one fabric piece using 1 strand of DMC ecru floss.

If needed, trim seam allowance of cording to 1/2"; pin cording to right side of pillow front, making a 3/8" clip in seam allowance of cording at corners. Ends of cording should overlap approximately 4". Turn overlapped ends of cording toward outside edge of pillow front; baste cording to pillow front.

Matching right sides and leaving an opening for turning, use a 1/2" seam allowance to sew pillow front and backing fabric together. Trim seam allowances diagonally at corners; turn pillow right side out, carefully pushing corners outward. Stuff pillow with polyester fiberfill and blind stitch opening closed.

pretty pillows

Angel Pillow (shown on page 10): The design was stitched over 2 fabric threads on a 7" x 9" piece of Charles Craft, Inc.® Cream Irish Linen (36 ct). Two strands of floss were used for Cross Stitch and 1 strand for Backstitch, unless otherwise noted in the color key.

For pillow, you will need tracing paper, pencil, fabric marking pencil, 18" length of ¹/₂" w braid, two 5" tassels, two 11" squares of fabric for pillow front and back, polyester fiberfill, and clear-drying craft glue.

For pattern, fold tracing paper in half and place fold on dashed line of pattern; trace pattern onto tracing paper. Cut out pattern; unfold and press flat. Referring to photo, position pattern on wrong side of stitched piece; pin pattern in place. Use fabric marking pencil to draw around pattern; remove pattern. Cut stitched piece ¹/₂" larger than pattern on all sides.

For pillow front, center stitched piece on one fabric piece; baste in place. Beginning at bottom center, glue braid around stitched piece, covering raw edges.

Matching right sides and raw edges and leaving an opening for turning, use a ¹/₂" seam allowance to sew pillow front and backing fabric together. Trim seam allowances diagonally at corners; turn pillow right side out, carefully pushing corners outward. Stuff pillow with polyester fiberfill and blind stitch opening closed.

Referring to photo, tack tassels to bottom corners of pillow.

Needlework adaptation by Carol Emmer.

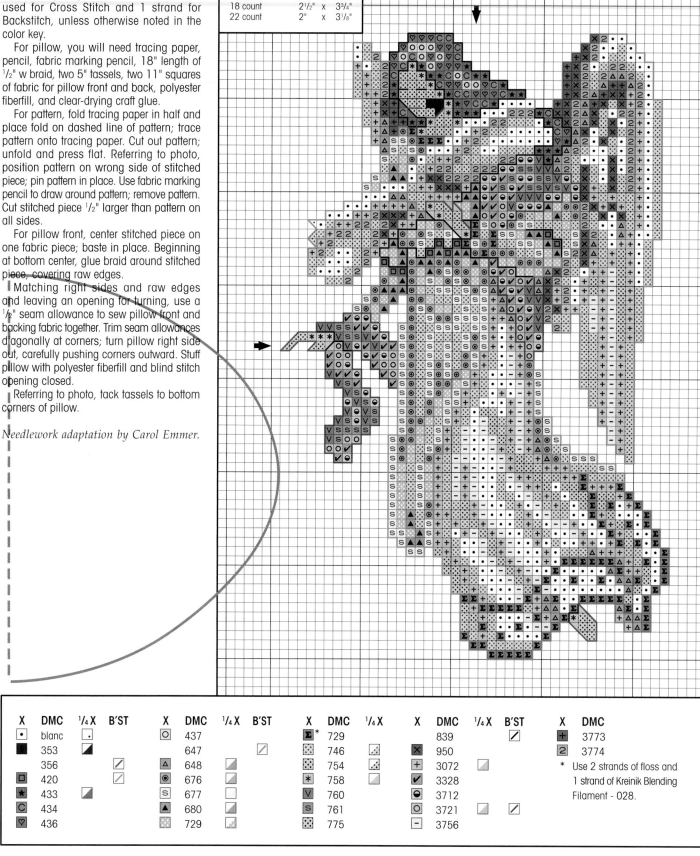

	STITCH COUNT (43w x 67h)	
14 count	3¹/₈"	x 4⁷/₈"
16 count	2³/₄"	x 4¹/₄"
18 count	2¹/₂"	x 3³/₄"
22 count	2"	x 3¹/₈"

X	DMC	¹/₄ X	B'ST	X	DMC	¹/₄ X	B'ST	X	DMC	¹/₄ X	X	DMC	¹/₄ X	B'ST	X	DMC
•	blanc	•		O	437			Σ*	729			839		/	+	3773
■	353	◪			647		/	746			✕	950			2	3774
	356		/	▲	648	/		754			+	3072	/			
▢	420	◪	/	◉	676	/		*	758	/	✔	3328				
★	433	◪		S	677	/		V	760		◑	3712				
C	434			▲	680	/		S	761		O	3721	/	/		
♡	436				729				775		-	3756				

* Use 2 strands of floss and 1 strand of Kreinik Blending Filament - 028.

52

GRANDFATHER FROST

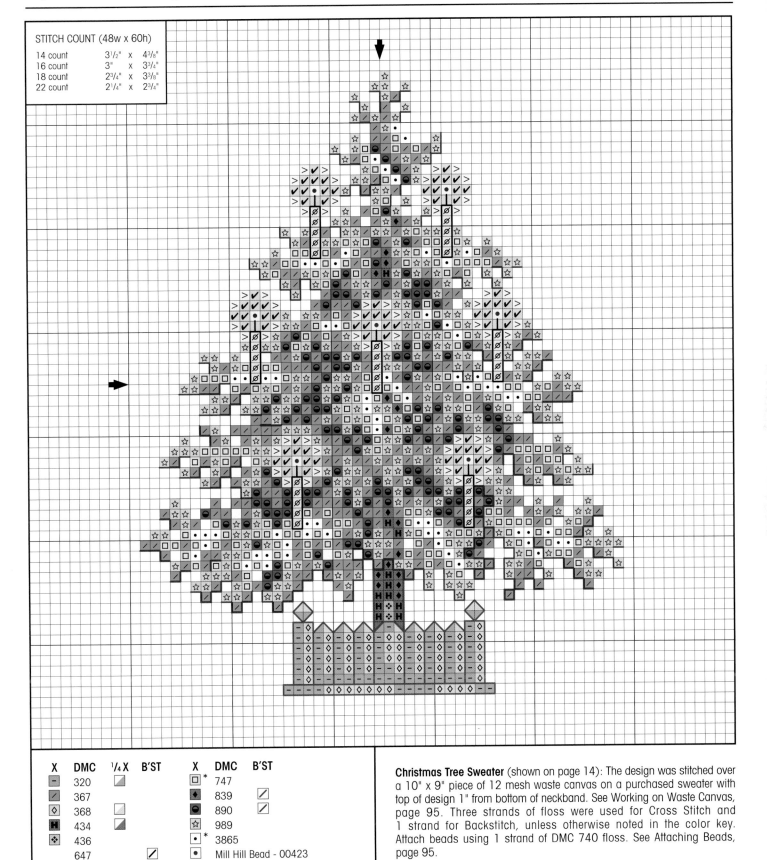

STITCH COUNT (48w x 60h)

14 count	3½"	x	4⅜"
16 count	3"	x	3¾"
18 count	2¾"	x	3⅜"
22 count	2¼"	x	2¾"

X	DMC	¼ X	B'ST		X	DMC	B'ST
−	320	◥			□*	747	
◢	367	◩			◆	839	◢
◇	368	◻			◑	890	◢
H	434	◪			☆	989	
❖	436				• *	3865	
	647		◢		•	Mill Hill Bead - 00423	
>	676						
✔	745				* Use 3 strands of floss and 2 strands		
∅	746				of Kreinik Blending Filament - 032.		

Christmas Tree Sweater (shown on page 14): The design was stitched over a 10" x 9" piece of 12 mesh waste canvas on a purchased sweater with top of design 1" from bottom of neckband. See Working on Waste Canvas, page 95. Three strands of floss were used for Cross Stitch and 1 strand for Backstitch, unless otherwise noted in the color key. Attach beads using 1 strand of DMC 740 floss. See Attaching Beads, page 95.

Design by Sandy Orton.

GRANDFATHER FROST

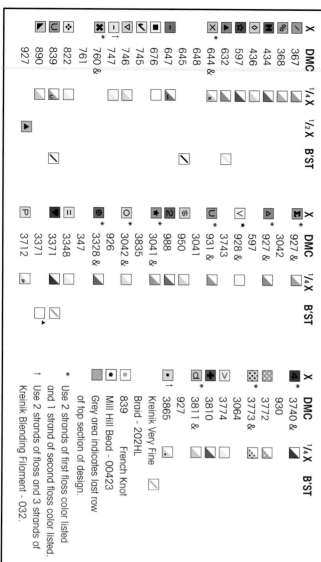

Grandfather Frost in Frame (shown on page 15): The design was stitched over 2 fabric threads on a 15" x 18" piece of Zweigart® Antique Ivory Cashel Linen® (28 ct). Three strands of floss were used for Cross Stitch and 1 strand for Half Cross Stitch, Backstitch, and French Knots, unless otherwise noted in the color key. Attach beads using 1 strand of DMC 676 floss. See Attaching Beads, page 95. It was custom framed.

Needlework adaptation by Sandy Orton.

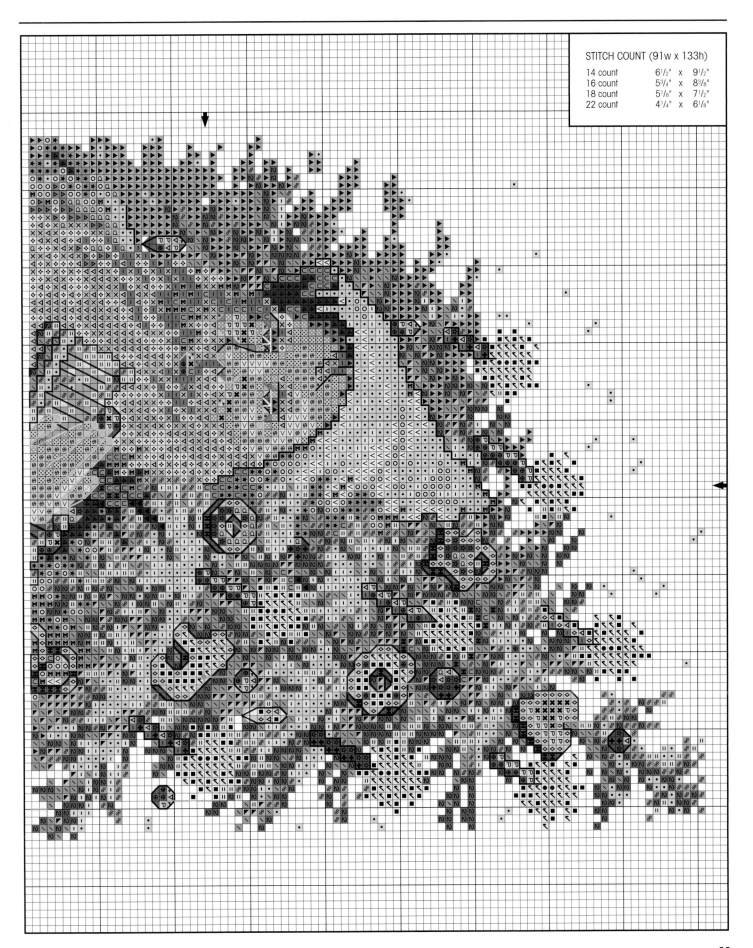

STITCH COUNT (91w x 133h)

14 count	6½" x	9½"
16 count	5¾" x	8⅜"
18 count	5⅛" x	7½"
22 count	4¼" x	6⅛"

WOODLAND CELEBRATION

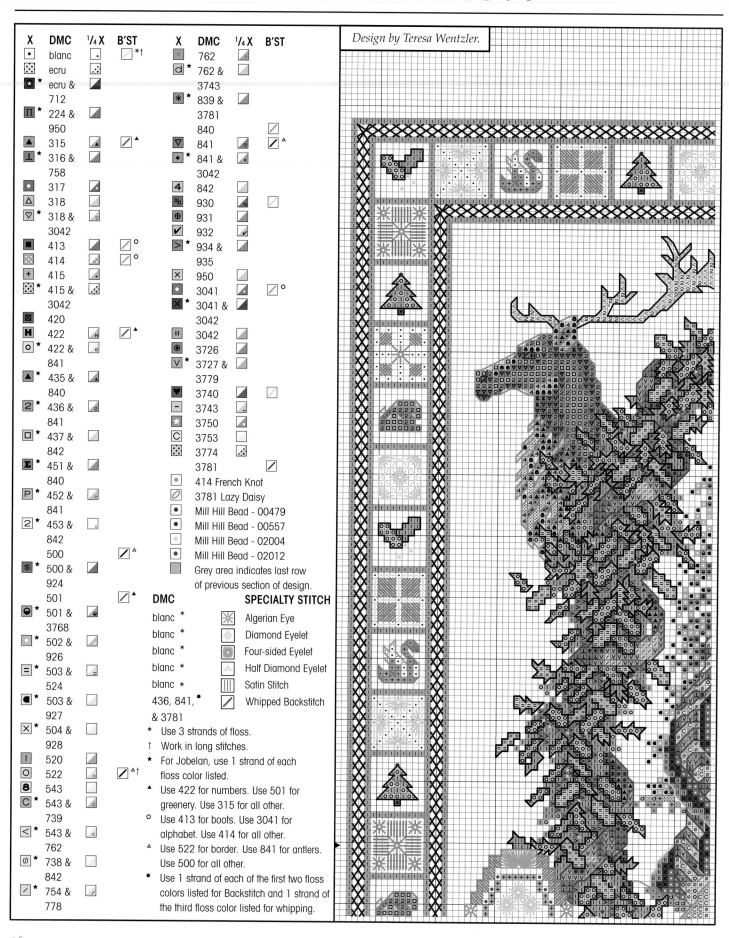

Design by Teresa Wentzler.

Color Key

X	DMC	1/4 X	B'ST
•	blanc	•	*†
	ecru		
★*	ecru & 712		
*	224 & 950		
▲	315	▲	▲
⊥*	316 & 758		
●	317		
△	318		
▽*	318 & 3042		
■	413		°
▨	414		°
+	415		
▦*	415 & 3042		
⊠	420		
H	422	H	▲
O*	422 & 841		
▲*	435 & 840		
2*	436 & 841		
▢*	437 & 842		
Σ*	451 & 840		
P*	452 & 841		
2*	453 & 842		
	500		△
$*	500 & 924		
	501		△
◐*	501 & 3768		
▫*	502 & 926		
=*	503 & 524		
◧*	503 & 927		
☒*	504 & 928		
▮	520		
O	522		
8	543		
C	543 & 739		
<*	543 & 762		
∅*	738 & 842		
◹*	754 & 778		
◎	762		
d*	762 & 3743		
✴*	839 & 3781		
	840		
▽	841	▽	△
◉	841 & 3042		
4	842		
%	930		
⊕	931		
✔	932	✔	
>*	934 & 935		
×	950		
◙	3041		°
⊠	3041 & 3042		
‖	3042		
◉	3726		
V	3727 & 3779		
◆	3740		
–	3743		
★	3750		
C	3753		
▩	3774		
	3781		

414 French Knot
3781 Lazy Daisy
Mill Hill Bead - 00479
Mill Hill Bead - 00557
Mill Hill Bead - 02004
Mill Hill Bead - 02012
Grey area indicates last row of previous section of design.

DMC	SPECIALTY STITCH
blanc *	Algerian Eye
blanc *	Diamond Eyelet
blanc *	Four-sided Eyelet
blanc *	Half Diamond Eyelet
blanc *	Satin Stitch
436, 841, & 3781 •	Whipped Backstitch

* Use 3 strands of floss.

† Work in long stitches.

★ For Jobelan, use 1 strand of each floss color listed.

▲ Use 422 for numbers. Use 501 for greenery. Use 315 for all other.

° Use 413 for boots. Use 3041 for alphabet. Use 414 for all other.

△ Use 522 for border. Use 841 for antlers. Use 500 for all other.

• Use 1 strand of each of the first two floss colors listed for Backstitch and 1 strand of the third floss color listed for whipping.

STITCH COUNT (178w x 237h)

14 count	12³/₄" x	17"
16 count	11¹/₈" x	14⁷/₈"
18 count	10" x	13¹/₄"
22 count	8¹/₈" x	10⁷/₈"

WOODLAND CELEBRATION

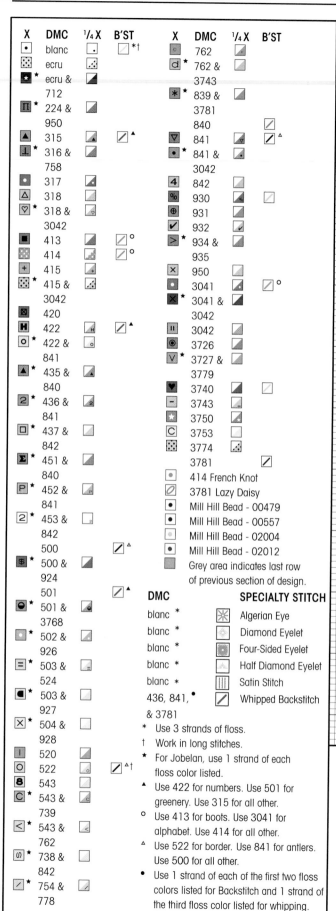

X	DMC	¼ X	B'ST		X	DMC	¼ X	B'ST
•	blanc		*†			762		
⋮	ecru				d★	762 &		
★*	ecru &					3743		
	712				*★	839 &		
Π*	224 &					3781		
	950					840		
▲	315			▲	▽	841		△
⊥*	316 &				•★	841 &		
	758					3042		
⊡	317				4	842		
△	318				%	930		
♡*	318 &				⊕	931		
	3042				✔	932		
■	413		°		▷*	934 &		
⊠	414		°			935		
+	415				×	950		
⊞*	415 &				◘	3041		°
	3042				✕★	3041 &		
⊠	420					3042		
H	422			▲	‖	3042		
O*	422 &				◎	3726		
	841				V*	3727 &		
▲*	435 &					3779		
	840				♥	3740		
2*	436 &				-	3743		
	841				⊡	3750		
□*	437 &				C	3753		
	842				⋮	3774		
Σ*	451 &					3781		
	840							
P*	452 &				⊙	414 French Knot		
	841				⊘	3781 Lazy Daisy		
2*	453 &				•	Mill Hill Bead - 00479		
	842				•	Mill Hill Bead - 00557		
	500		△		•	Mill Hill Bead - 02004		
$*	500 &				•	Mill Hill Bead - 02012		
	924							

Grey area indicates last row of previous section of design.

X	DMC	¼ X	B'ST
	501		△
◐*	501 &		
	3768		
⊡*	502 &		
	926		
=*	503 &		
	524		
◖*	503 &		
	927		
X*	504 &		
	928		
I	520		
O	522		△†
8	543		
C*	543 &		
	739		
<*	543 &		
	762		
⊚*	738 &		
	842		
⊘*	754 &		
	778		

DMC
blanc *
blanc *
blanc *
blanc *
blanc *
436, 841,
& 3781

SPECIALTY STITCH
✳ Algerian Eye
✺ Diamond Eyelet
◉ Four-Sided Eyelet
⬙ Half Diamond Eyelet
‖‖‖ Satin Stitch
⊘ Whipped Backstitch

* Use 3 strands of floss.
† Work in long stitches.
★ For Jobelan, use 1 strand of each floss color listed.
▲ Use 422 for numbers. Use 501 for greenery. Use 315 for all other.
° Use 413 for boots. Use 3041 for alphabet. Use 414 for all other.
△ Use 522 for border. Use 841 for antlers. Use 500 for all other.
• Use 1 strand of each of the first two floss colors listed for Backstitch and 1 strand of the third floss color listed for whipping.

Father Winter in Frame (shown on page 17): The design was stitched over 2 fabric threads on a 21" x 25" piece of Antique White Jobelan (28 ct). Two strands of floss were used for Cross Stitch and French Knots and 1 strand for Backstitch and Lazy Daisy Stitches, unless otherwise noted in the color key. Refer to chart for type of thread and number of strands used for Specialty Stitches. See Specialty Stitch Diagrams, page 96. Attach beads using 1 strand of DMC blanc floss for white beads, 1 strand of DMC 422 floss for gold beads, and 1 strand of DMC 316 floss for plum and rose beads. See Attaching Beads, page 95. Personalize and date design using DMC 414 floss and alphabet and numerals provided. It was custom framed.

Father Winter Afghan (shown on page 18): A portion of the design (refer to photo) was stitched over 2 fabric threads on a 45" x 58" piece of White All-Cotton

center year

Anne Cloth (18 ct). Refer to diagram, page 81, for placement of design on fabric; use 6 strands of floss for Cross Stitch and 2 strands for Backstitch, French Knots, and Lazy Daisy Stitches. For blended floss colors, use 3 strands of each floss color listed. To complete afghan, see Finishing Instructions, page 81.

Woodland Border Candle Band (shown on page 19): A portion of the design (refer to photo) was stitched over 2 fabric threads on an 18" x 6" piece of Zweigart® Antique White Lugana (25 ct). Three strands of floss were used for Cross Stitch and 1 strand for Backstitch, unless otherwise noted in the color key. For blended floss colors, use 2 strands of first floss color listed and 1 strand of second floss color listed. Refer to chart for type of thread and number of strands used for Specialty Stitches. See Specialty Stitch Diagrams, page 96.

Centering design, trim stitched piece to measure 16" x 4".
Matching right sides and long edges fold stitched piece in half. Using a ¼" seam allowance, sew long edges together; trim seam allowance to ⅛" and turn stitched piece right side out. With seam centered in back, press stitched piece flat.
Wrap candle band around candle, turning raw edges to wrong side so that ends meet; blind stitch short ends together.

Woodland Border Ornaments (shown on page 16): Portions of the design (refer to photo) were each stitched over 2 fabric threads on a 6" square of Zweigart® Moss Green Lugana (25 ct). Three strands of floss were used for Cross Stitch and Backstitch. Refer to chart for type of thread and number of strands used for Specialty Stitches. See Specialty Stitch Diagrams, page 96. To complete ornaments, see Finishing Instructions, page 81.

59

NOSTALGIC TOUCHES

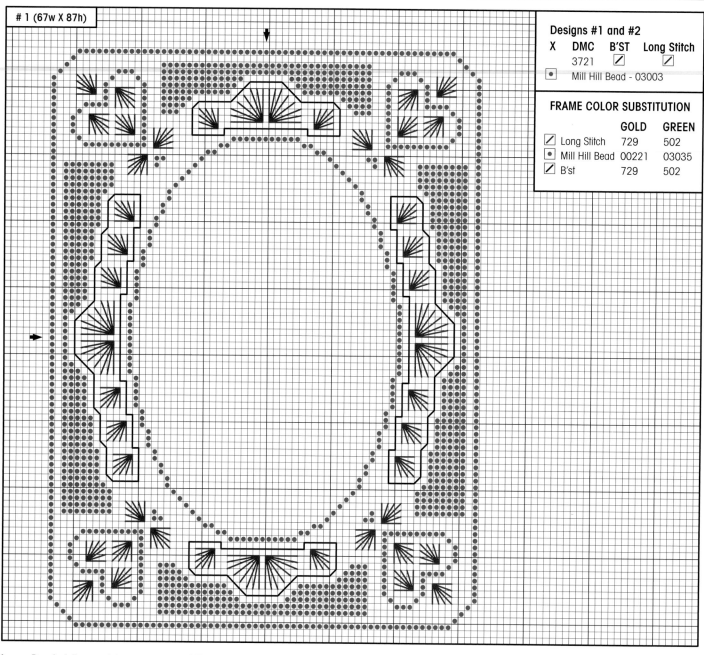

 # 1 (67w X 87h)

Designs #1 and #2

X	DMC	B'ST	Long Stitch
	3721	⟋	⟋
⊙	Mill Hill Bead - 03003		

FRAME COLOR SUBSTITUTION

		GOLD	GREEN
⟋	Long Stitch	729	502
⊙	Mill Hill Bead	00221	03035
⟋	B'st	729	502

Large Beaded Frame (shown on page 20) and **Small Beaded Frames** (shown on page 21): Each design was stitched using 2 strands of floss for Long Stitch and Backstitch. Attach beads using 1 strand of floss. See Attaching Beads, page 95. Design #1 was stitched on a 7" x 8" piece of Brown perforated paper (14 ct). Design #2 was stitched on a 6" x 7" piece of Brown perforated paper (14 ct). Refer to chart for color substitution list.

For frame, you will need Brown perforated paper and clear-drying craft glue.

Referring to photo, trim frame close to inner and outer edges of stitched design.

For frame backing, cut one piece of perforated paper ¹/₄" larger on all sides than desired photo measurement. Center backing on wrong side of photo frame and glue side and bottom edges in place.

Designs by Kathy Elrod.

Nostalgic Ornaments Pattern

2 (57w X 73h)

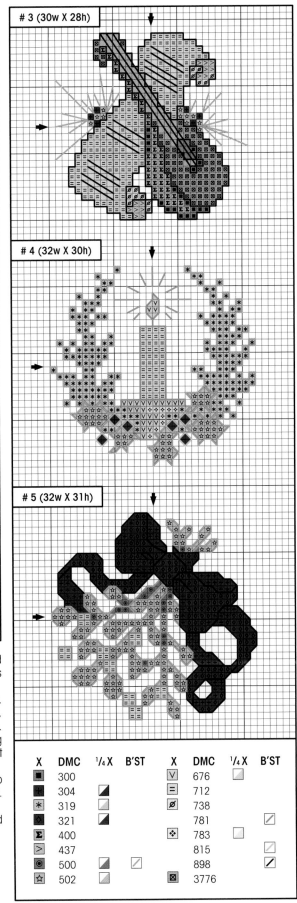

3 (30w X 28h)

4 (32w X 30h)

5 (32w X 31h)

Nostalgic Ornaments (shown on page 20-21): Designs #3, #4, and #5 were each stitched over 2 fabric threads on a 7" square of Zweigart® Cream Belfast Linen (32 ct). Two strands of floss were used for Cross Stitch and 1 strand for Backstitch.

For each ornament, you will need tracing paper, pencil, fabric marking pencil, 3" dia. Styrofoam® ball, 7" x 11" piece of Cream Belfast Linen, 20" length of ¼"w braid, 3" tassel, 3 assorted beads, 10" length of narrow cord for hanger, and clear-drying craft glue.

Trace pattern, page 60, onto tracing paper; cut out pattern. Centering pattern on wrong side of stitched piece, draw around pattern with fabric marking pencil; cut out shape. Repeat 3 times with piece of linen.

Apply glue to **edges only** on wrong side of stitched piece; smooth and press edges onto ball. Matching points and aligning raw edges, continue gluing fabric pieces around ball. Referring to photo, glue braid over raw edges of fabric pieces.

For hanger, fold cord in half; knot ends together. Referring to photo, thread folded end through beads. Glue hanger to top of ornament and tassel to bottom of ornament.

Designs by Holly DeFount.

X	DMC	¼ X	B'ST	X	DMC	¼ X	B'ST
■	300			V	676		
✚	304	◢		=	712	◢	
✱	319	◢		∅	738		
◆	321	◢		❖	781		◢
Σ	400			❖	783	◢	
>	437				815		◢
◉	500	◢	◢		898		◢
☆	502	◢		⊠	3776		

TIDINGS FROM ABOVE

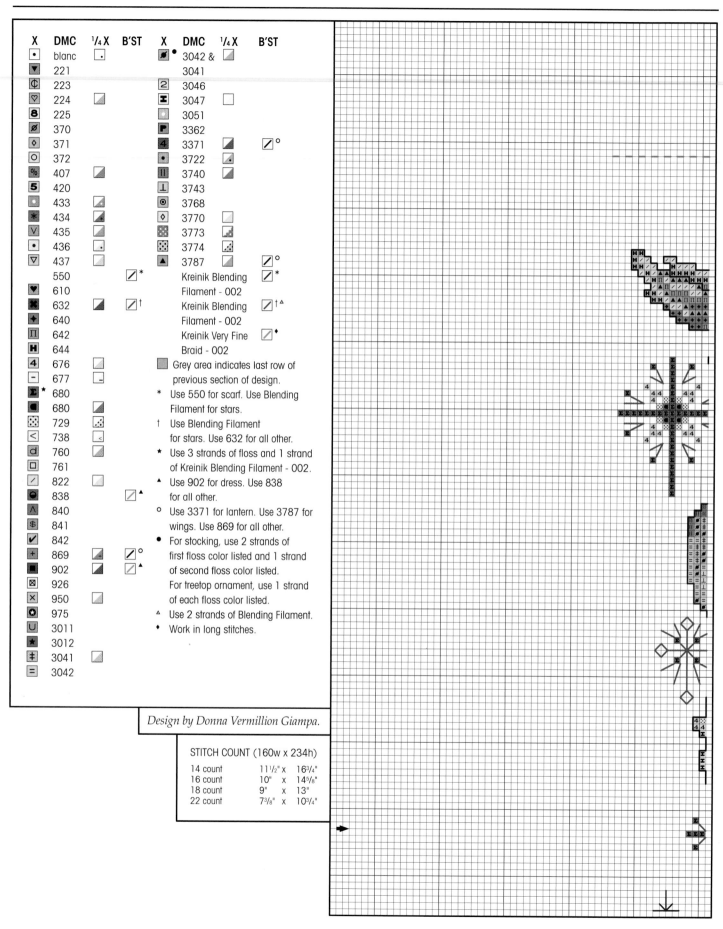

X	DMC	¼X	B'ST	X	DMC	¼X	B'ST
•	blanc	•			3042 &		
▼	221				3041		
₵	223			2	3046		
▽	224			✕	3047	☐	
8	225				3051		
∅	370			P	3362		
◇	371			4	3371		∕°
○	372			•	3722		
%	407			‖	3740		
5	420			⊥	3743		
▣	433			⊙	3768		
✱	434			◇	3770	☐	
V	435			⁘	3773		
•	436	•		⁙	3774		
▽	437			▲	3787		∕°
	550		∕*		Kreinik Blending		∕*
♥	610				Filament - 002		
✖	632		∕†		Kreinik Blending		∕†△
◆	640				Filament - 002		
Π	642				Kreinik Very Fine		∕◆
H	644				Braid - 002		
4	676						
-	677	-			Grey area indicates last row of		
Σ★	680				previous section of design.		
◖	680						
⁂	729			*	Use 550 for scarf. Use Blending		
<	738	<			Filament for stars.		
◗	760			†	Use Blending Filament		
▢	761				for stars. Use 632 for all other.		
∕	822	☐		★	Use 3 strands of floss and 1 strand		
◕	838		∕△		of Kreinik Blending Filament - 002.		
∧	840			▲	Use 902 for dress. Use 838		
$	841				for all other.		
✔	842			°	Use 3371 for lantern. Use 3787 for		
+	869		∕°		wings. Use 869 for all other.		
■	902		∕△	•	For stocking, use 2 strands of		
⊠	926				first floss color listed and 1 strand		
✕	950				of second floss color listed.		
◉	975				For treetop ornament, use 1 strand		
U	3011				of each floss color listed.		
★	3012			△	Use 2 strands of Blending Filament.		
‡	3041			◆	Work in long stitches.		
=	3042						

Design by Donna Vermillion Giampa.

STITCH COUNT (160w x 234h)

14 count	11½" x	16¾"
16 count	10" x	14⅝"
18 count	9" x	13"
22 count	7⅜" x	10¾"

center name

TIDINGS FROM ABOVE

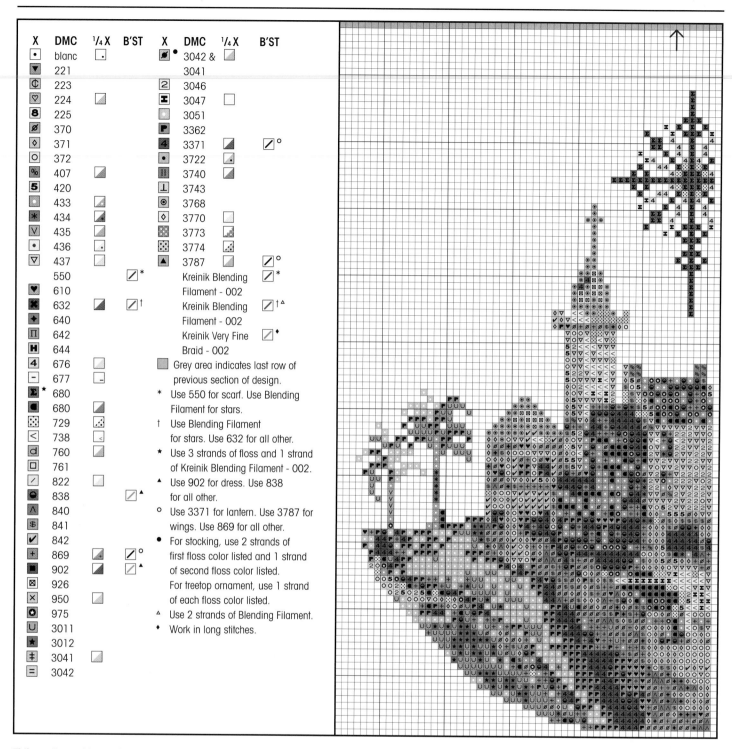

X	DMC	¼X	B'ST	X	DMC	¼X	B'ST
•	blanc	•		◩	3042 &		◩
▼	221				3041		
₵	223			2	3046		
▽	224	◩		⊞	3047	□	
8	225			▣	3051		
∅	370			P	3362		
◇	371			4	3371	◩	◩°
O	372			•	3722		
%	407	◩		‖	3740	◩	
5	420			⊥	3743		
▢	433	◩		◉	3768		
✳	434	◪		◇	3770		◩
V	435			▨	3773		◪
•	436	•		⊠	3774	∷	
▽	437	◩		▲	3787		◩°
	550		◩*		Kreinik Blending		◩*
♥	610				Filament - 002		
✖	632	◪	◩†		Kreinik Blending		◩†△
✦	640				Filament - 002		
Π	642				Kreinik Very Fine		◩♦
H	644				Braid - 002		
4	676	□		▣	Grey area indicates last row of		
−	677	−			previous section of design.		
Σ*	680			*	Use 550 for scarf. Use Blending		
◼	680	◪			Filament for stars.		
⠿	729	∷		†	Use Blending Filament		
<	738	<			for stars. Use 632 for all other.		
d	760	◩		★	Use 3 strands of floss and 1 strand		
▢	761				of Kreinik Blending Filament - 002.		
◢	822	□		▲	Use 902 for dress. Use 838		
◕	838		◩▲		for all other.		
∧	840			°	Use 3371 for lantern. Use 3787 for		
$	841				wings. Use 869 for all other.		
✔	842			•	For stocking, use 2 strands of		
+	869	◪	◩°		first floss color listed and 1 strand		
■	902	◩	◩▲		of second floss color listed.		
⊠	926	◩			For treetop ornament, use 1 strand		
×	950	◩			of each floss color listed.		
✿	975			△	Use 2 strands of Blending Filament.		
U	3011			♦	Work in long stitches.		
★	3012						
‡	3041	◩					
=	3042						

Tidings From Above Stocking (shown on page 13): The design was stitched on a 19" x 23" piece of Charles Craft, Inc.® Navy Aida (14 ct). Three strands of floss were used for Cross Stitch and 1 strand for Backstitch, unless otherwise noted in the color key. Personalize stocking using alphabet provided, page 66.

For stocking, you will need a 19" x 23" piece of fabric for backing, two 19" x 23" pieces of fabric for lining, 68" length of ¼" dia. purchased cord for stocking, 8" length of ¼" dia. purchased cord for hanger, tracing paper, and fabric marking pencil.

For pattern, photocopy the Stocking Pattern, page 66, enlarging it 130%. Match arrows of pattern to form one pattern and trace pattern onto tracing paper; add a ½" seam allowance on all sides and cut out pattern. Referring to photo for placement, position pattern on wrong side of stitched

piece; pin pattern in place. Use fabric marking pencil to draw around pattern; remove pattern and cut **one** from backing fabric and **two** from lining fabric.

Matching right sides and leaving top edge open, use a ½" seam allowance to sew stitched piece and backing fabric together. Clip seam allowance at curves and turn stocking right side out. Press top edge of stocking 1" to wrong side.

Matching right sides and leaving top edge open, use a ⅝" seam allowance to sew lining pieces together; trim seam allowance close to stitching. **Do not turn lining right side out.** Press top of lining 1" to wrong side. With wrong sides facing, place lining inside stocking; blind stitch lining to stocking.

Referring to photo, whipstitch cord to top, bottom, and side edges

Design by Donna Vermillion Giampa.

of stocking.

For hanger, fold cord in half and whipstitch to inside of stocking at right seam.

Celestial Treetop Ornament (shown on page 12): A portion of the design (refer to photo) was stitched on a 16" x 19" piece of Charles Craft, Inc.® Smoke Aida (14 ct). Two strands of floss were used for Cross Stitch and 1 strand for Backstitch, unless otherwise noted in the color key.

For treetop ornament, you will need a 16" x 19" piece of Smoke Aida for backing, polyester fiberfill, and two 18" lengths of ¼"w ribbon for ties.

Matching right sides and raw edges and leaving an opening for turning, sew stitched piece and backing fabric together 2 squares from edge of design. Trim seam allowance to ¼". Clip seam allowances at curves; turn

treetop ornament right side out; carefully pushing curves outward. Stuff treetop ornament with polyester fiberfill; blind stitch opening closed.

For ties, fold each ribbon length in half and tack center of each length to back of treetop ornament 4" apart (**Fig. 1**).

Fig. 1

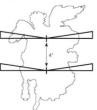

65

TIDINGS FROM ABOVE

X	DMC
⊠	729

Stocking Top Pattern

Stocking Bottom Pattern

YULETIDE TOYS

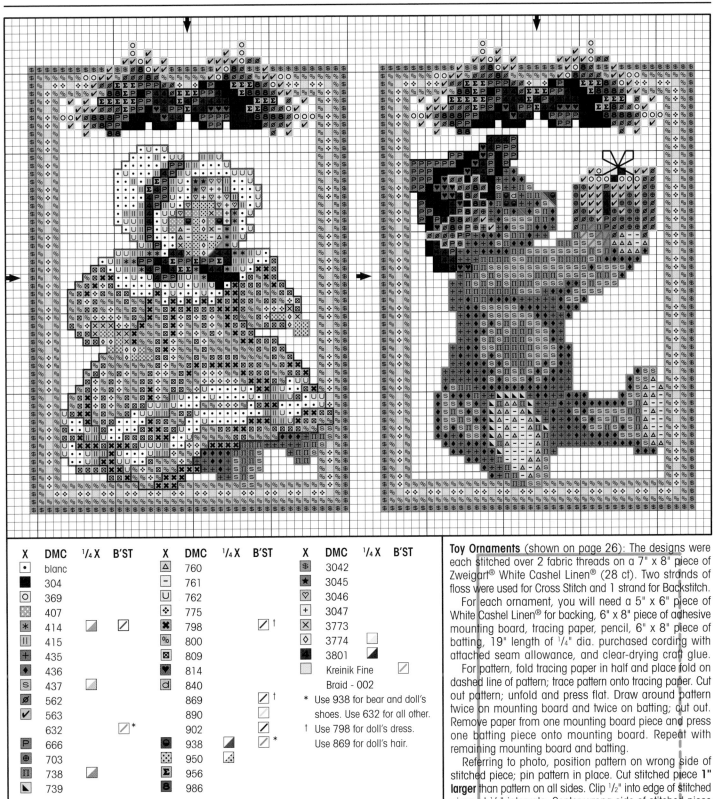

X	DMC	¼ X	B'ST	X	DMC	¼ X	B'ST	X	DMC	¼ X	B'ST
•	blanc			△	760			$	3042		
■	304			–	761			★	3045		
○	369			U	762			♡	3046		
▧	407			✧	775			+	3047		
✱	414	◪	◪	✖	798		◪ †	✕	3773		
‖	415			%	800			◇	3774		◪
✚	435			⊠	809			◼	3801	◪	◼
◆	436			♥	814				Kreinik Fine		◪
S	437	◪		d	840				Braid - 002		
⌀	562				869		◪ †				
✔	563				890		◪	* Use 938 for bear and doll's			
	632		◪ *		902		◪	shoes. Use 632 for all other.			
P	666			⬢	938	◪	◪ *	† Use 798 for doll's dress.			
⊕	703			⬡	950	⬓		Use 869 for doll's hair.			
Π	738	◪		Σ	956						
◣	739			⊟	986						

Designs by Donna Vermillion Giampa.

STITCH COUNT (41w x 59h)

14 count	3"	x 4¼"
16 count	2⅝"	x 3¾"
18 count	2⅜"	x 3⅜"
22 count	1⅞"	x 2¾"

Toy Ornaments (shown on page 26): The designs were each stitched over 2 fabric threads on a 7" x 8" piece of Zweigart® White Cashel Linen® (28 ct). Two strands of floss were used for Cross Stitch and 1 strand for Backstitch.

For each ornament, you will need a 5" x 6" piece of White Cashel Linen® for backing, 6" x 8" piece of adhesive mounting board, tracing paper, pencil, 6" x 8" piece of batting, 19" length of ¼" dia. purchased cording with attached seam allowance, and clear-drying craft glue.

For pattern, fold tracing paper in half and place fold on dashed line of pattern; trace pattern onto tracing paper. Cut out pattern; unfold and press flat. Draw around pattern twice on mounting board and twice on batting; cut out. Remove paper from one mounting board piece and press one batting piece onto mounting board. Repeat with remaining mounting board and batting.

Referring to photo, position pattern on wrong side of stitched piece; pin pattern in place. Cut stitched piece **1" larger** than pattern on all sides. Clip ½" into edge of stitched piece at ½" intervals. Center wrong side of stitched piece over batting on mounting board piece; fold edges of stitched piece to back of mounting board and glue in place. For ornament back, repeat with backing fabric and remaining mounting board.

Beginning and ending at bottom center of stitched piece, glue cording seam allowance to wrong side of ornament front, overlapping ends of cording. Matching wrong sides, glue ornament front and back together.

X	DMC	¼ X	B'ST	X	DMC	¼ X	B'ST
•	blanc	•	☑ *	✿	816	◪	
2	ecru	◻		☆	822	◪	
T	300	◪		•	839	◪	
◉	309	◪		■	902	◪	☐ †
‖	312	◪		♡	913	◪	
	317	☑ *		•	935	◪	☑ *
✿	318	◪		✾	938	◪	☑
■	321	◪		✕	950	◪	
⊕	322	◪		◉	3031	◪	
◉	335	◪		4	3032	◪	
■	336	◪	☐ †	✔	3047	◪	
♥	350	◪		✹	3328	◪	
▽	351	◪		○	3345	◪	
%	352	◻		◻	3347	◪	
◥	355	◪		‖	3348	◻	
◉	415	◪			3371		☑
▼	433	◪		P	3712	◪	
✕	435	◪		◥	3713	◪	
$	437	◪		<	3753	◻	
■	500	☑		◿	3755	◪	
⊞	561	◪		◇	3770	◪	
Π	562	◪		☰	3772	◪	
U	564	◪		d	3773	◪	
⊞	632	◪	☐ †	▥	3774	◪	
◆	642	◪		∧	3782	◪	
>	644	◻			3787		☑ *
d	676	◻		◈	3790	◪	
★	680	◪					
4 ▲	725	◻					
Σ	729	◪					
+	738	+					
-	760	◪					
5	761	◻					
✖	762	◻					
●	772	◻					
H ▲	780	◪					
∩	781	◻	☑ *				
∅	781	◻					
◼	783						
✤ ▲	783	◻					
⊠	801	◪	☑				
C	813	◪					
✳	814	◪					

■ Grey area indicates last row of previous section of design.

* Use blanc for eyes. Use 781 for stems. Use 317 for all other.

† Use 632 for doll's face and hands. Use 902 for red ribbon and berries. Use 336 for all other.

▲ Use 2 strands of floss and 1 strand of Kreinik Blending Filament - 002.

★ Use 3787 for hair and beard. Use 935 for all other.

STITCH COUNT (141w x 216h)

14 count	10⅛"	x	15½"	
16 count	8⅞"	x	13½"	
18 count	7⅞"	x	12"	
22 count	6½"	x	9⅞"	

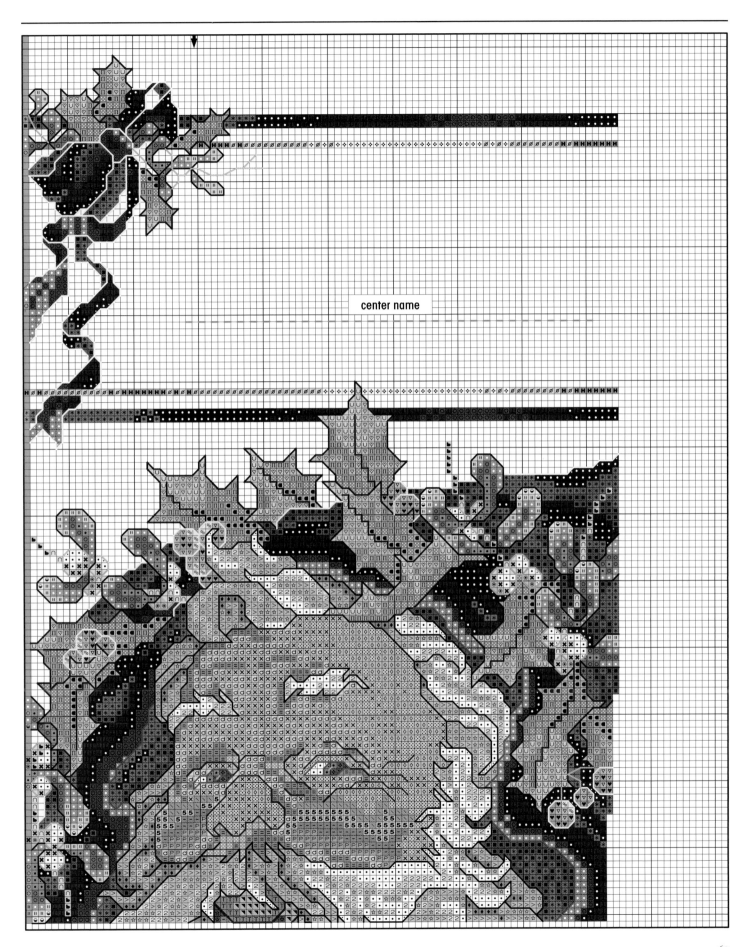

center name

X	DMC	1/4 X	B'ST		X	DMC	1/4 X	B'ST
•	blanc	•	✦ *		•	816	◣	
2	ecru				☆	822	◥	
T	300	◣			•	839	◣	
◎	309	◣			■	902	◣	☐ †
‖	312	◥			♡	913	◥	
	317	◢ *			●	935	◣	✦ ★
✪	318	◣			●	938	◣	◢
■	321	◤			X	950	◥	
⊕	322	◥			◙	3031	◣	
◈	335	◣			4	3032	◥	
◢	336	◤	☐ †		✔	3047	◣	
♥	350	◥			✱	3328	◣	
▽	351	▽			◉	3345	◥	
%	352				◐	3347	◥	
◣	355	◥			‖	3348	◥	
◉	415	◥				3371		◢
▼	433	◢			P	3712	◥	
X	435	◥			◣	3713	◥	
$	437	◥			<	3753	◥	
◖	500	◣	◢		/	3755	◥	
◙	561	◣			◈	3770	◇	
Π	562	◥			=	3772	◥	
U	564	◥			d	3773	◥	
◙	632	◣	☐ †		⬚	3774	⬚	
◆	642	◥			∧	3782	◥	
>	644	◥				3787		◢ ★
d	676	◥			◆	3790	◥	
★	680	◥						
4 ▲	725							
Σ	729	◥						
+	738	+						
-	760	◣						
5	761	◥						
✱	762	◥						
◎	772	◥						
H ▲	780	◥						
∩	781	◥	◢ *					
ø ▲	781	◥						
◧	783	◥						
⬗ ▲	783							
▩	801	◣	◢					
C	813	◥						
✳	814	◣						

◼ Grey area indicates last row of
previous section of design.

* Use blanc for eyes. Use 781
for stems. Use 317 for all other.

† Use 632 for doll's face and hands.
Use 902 for red ribbon and berries.
Use 336 for all other.

▲ Use 2 strands of floss and 1 strand
of Kreinik Blending Filament - 002.

★ Use 3787 for hair and beard.
Use 935 for all other.

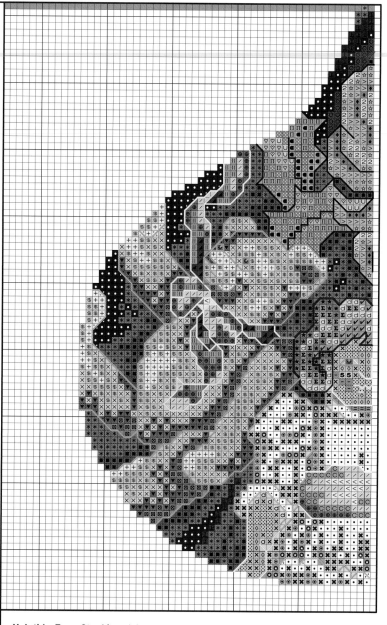

Yuletide Toys Stocking (shown on page 27): The design was stitched over 2 fabric threads on an 18" x 24" piece of Zweigart® White Cashel Linen® (28 ct). Two strands of floss were used for Cross Stitch and 1 strand for Backstitch. Personalize stocking using alphabet on page 94.

For stocking, you will need an 18" x 24" piece of fabric for backing, two 18" x 24" pieces of fabric for lining, 44" length of ¼" dia. purchased cording with attached seam allowance, 2" x 7" length of fabric for hanger, tracing paper, and fabric marking pencil.

Matching arrows of Stocking Pattern (page 80) to form one pattern, trace pattern onto tracing paper; add a ½" seam allowance on all sides and cut out pattern. Referring to photo for placement, position pattern on wrong side of stitched

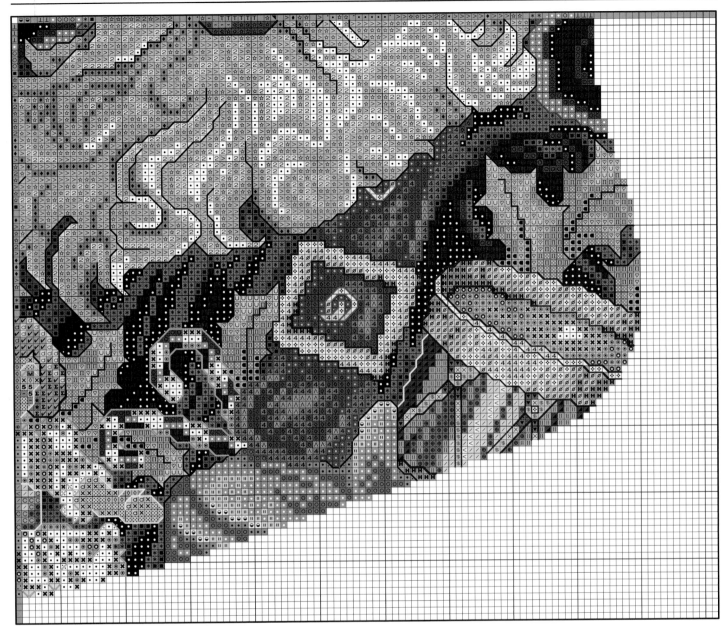

piece; pin pattern in place. Use fabric marking pencil to draw around pattern; remove pattern and cut out on drawn line. Use pattern and cut **one** from backing fabric and **two** from lining fabric.

If needed, trim seam allowance of cording to $1/2$". Matching raw edges, baste cording to right side of stocking front.

Matching right sides and leaving top edge open, use a $1/2$" seam allowance to sew stitched piece and backing fabric together. Clip seam allowance at curves and turn stocking right side out. Press top edge of stocking $1/2$" to wrong side.

Matching right sides and leaving top edge open, use a $5/8$" seam allowance to sew lining pieces together; trim seam allowance close to stitching.

Do not turn lining right side out. Press top edge of lining $1/2$" to wrong side.

For hanger, press each long edge of fabric strip $1/2$" to center. Matching long edges, fold strip in half and sew close to folded edges. Matching short edges, fold hanger in half and whipstitch to inside of stocking at right seam.

With wrong sides facing, place lining inside stocking; blind stitch lining to stocking.

Design by Donna Vermillion Giampa.

MERRY GENTLEMEN

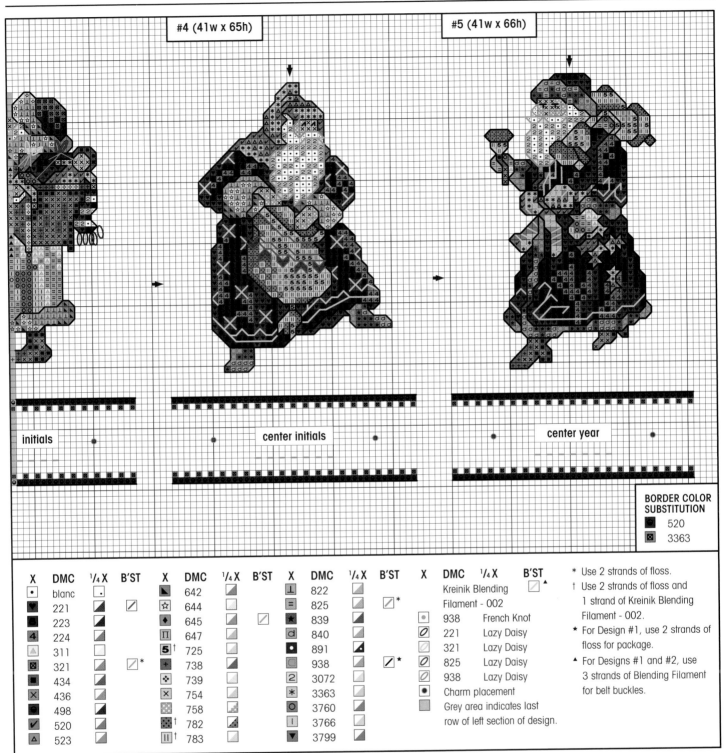

#4 (41w x 65h)   #5 (41w x 66h)

initials   center initials   center year

BORDER COLOR SUBSTITUTION
520
3363

X	DMC	¹/₄ X	B'ST	X	DMC	¹/₄ X	B'ST	X	DMC	¹/₄ X	B'ST	X	DMC	¹/₄ X	B'ST
•	blanc	•			642				822				Kreinik Blending		▲
	221			☆	644			=	825		✓*		Filament - 002		
	223			◆	645		✓	★	839			•	938	French Knot	
4	224			Π	647			d	840			∅	221	Lazy Daisy	
△	311			5	725	†		●	891			∅	321	Lazy Daisy	
⊠	321		✓*		738			◐	938		✓*	∅	825	Lazy Daisy	
■	434			❖	739			2	3072			∅	938	Lazy Daisy	
×	436			×	754			*	3363			•	Charm placement		
●	498				758	†		○	3760				Grey area indicates last		
✓	520				782	†		I	3766				row of left section of design.		
△	523			II	783	†		▼	3799						

* Use 2 strands of floss.

† Use 2 strands of floss and 1 strand of Kreinik Blending Filament - 002.

★ For Design #1, use 2 strands of floss for package.

▲ For Designs #1 and #2, use 3 strands of Blending Filament for belt buckles.

Merry Gentlemen Ornaments (shown on pages 28-29): Each design was stitched over 2 fabric threads on a 7" x 9" piece of Zweigart® White Cashel Linen® (28 ct). Two strands of floss were used for Cross Stitch and Lazy Daisy Stitches and 1 strand for Backstitch and French Knots, unless otherwise noted in the color key. Attach charms using 1 strand of DMC blanc floss. Personalize and date designs using alphabet and numerals provided.

For each ornament, you will need a 10" length of ¹/₈" dia. cord for hanger.

Trim stitched piece to measure 6¹/₂" x 7" allowing a ³/₄" margin at bottom of design, a 1¹/₂" margin at sides of design, and a 1³/₄" margin at top of design.

Machine stitch ¹/₂" from bottom edge of stitched piece; fringe to within 1 fabric thread of stitching. Matching right sides and long edges, fold stitched piece in half. Using a ¹/₄" seam allowance, sew long edges together; trim seam allowance to ¹/₈" and turn stitched piece right side out. With seam centered in back, press stitched piece flat. Referring to photo, fold top edge of stitched piece to wrong side to form a casing; whipstitch in place. Thread cord through casing. Use an overhand knot to tie ends of cord together; position knot inside casing.

Designs by Donna Vermillion Giampa.

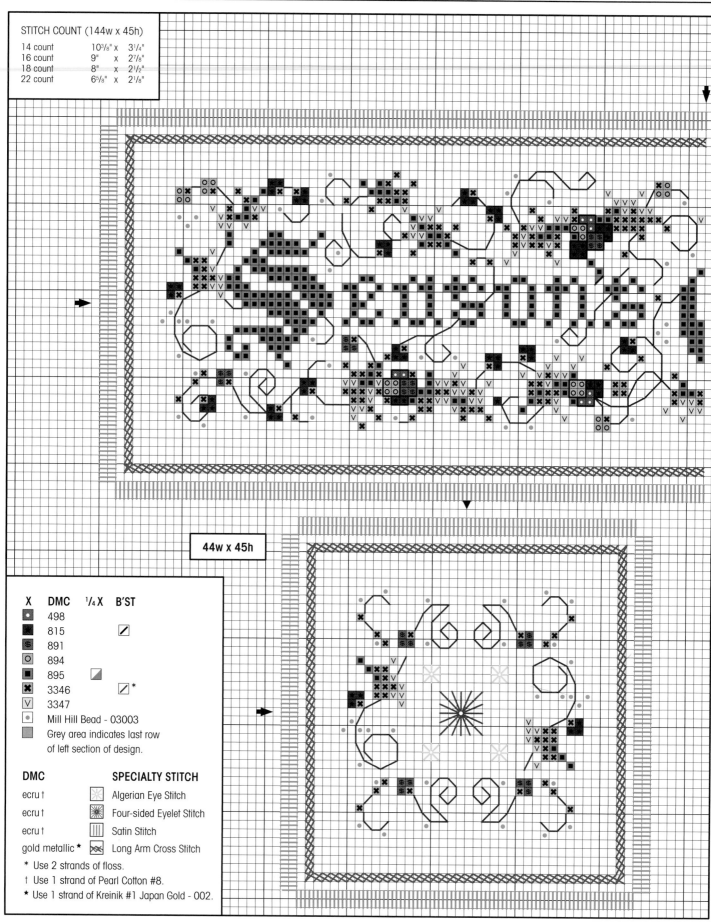

STITCH COUNT (144w x 45h)

14 count	10³/₈"	x	3¹/₄"
16 count	9"	x	2⁷/₈"
18 count	8"	x	2¹/₂"
22 count	6⁵/₈"	x	2¹/₈"

44w x 45h

X	DMC	¹/₄X	B'ST
▢	498		
✳	815		◢
$	891		
○	894		
▪	895	◩	
✖	3346		◢ *
V	3347		
•	Mill Hill Bead - 03003		
▨	Grey area indicates last row of left section of design.		

DMC		SPECIALTY STITCH
ecru †	✳	Algerian Eye Stitch
ecru †	✳	Four-sided Eyelet Stitch
ecru †	▥	Satin Stitch
gold metallic ✱	⧅	Long Arm Cross Stitch

* Use 2 strands of floss.
† Use 1 strand of Pearl Cotton #8.
✱ Use 1 strand of Kreinik #1 Japan Gold - 002.

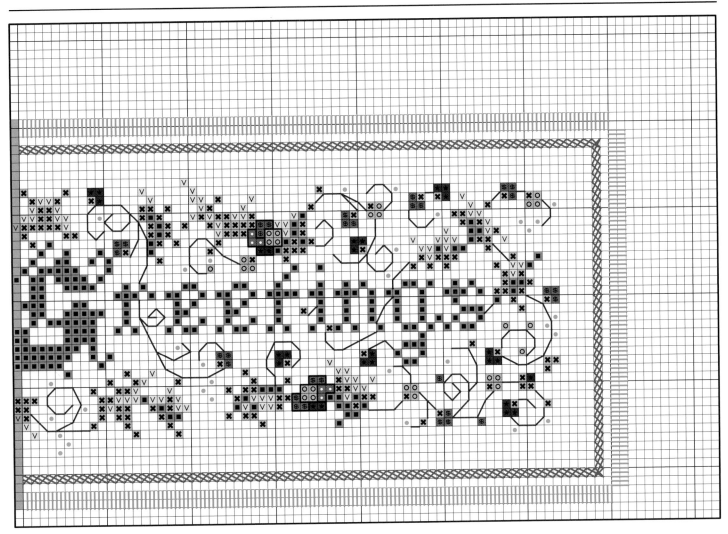

Season's Greetings in Frame (shown on page 31): The design was stitched over 2 fabric threads on a 17" x 11" piece of Zweigart® Cream Belfast Linen (32 ct). Two strands of floss were used for Cross Stitch and 1 strand for Backstitch, unless otherwise noted in the color key. Refer to chart for type of thread and number of strands used for Specialty Stitches. See Specialty Stitch Diagrams, page 96. Attach beads using 1 strand of DMC 815 floss. See Attaching Beads, page 95. It was custom framed.

Holiday Border Ornament (shown on page 30): The design was stitched over 2 fabric threads on a 7" square of Zweigart® Cream Belfast Linen (32 ct). Two strands of floss were used for Cross Stitch and 1 strand for Backstitch, unless otherwise noted in the color key. Refer to chart for type of thread and number of strands used for Specialty Stitches. See Specialty Stitch Diagrams, page 95. Attach beads using 1 strand of DMC 815 floss. See Attaching Beads, page 95.

For ornament, you will need a 7" square of Cream Belfast Linen for backing, two 3½" squares of adhesive mounting board, two 3½" squares of batting, 16" length of ¼" dia. purchased cording with attached seam allowance,

7" length of ¼" dia. cord for hanger, 2" tassel, and clear-drying craft glue.

Centering design, trim stitched piece to measure 5½" square.

Remove paper from one mounting board piece and press one batting piece onto mounting board. Repeat with remaining mounting board and batting.

Clip ½" into edge of stitched piece at ½" intervals. Center wrong side of stitched piece over batting on one mounting board piece; fold edges of stitched piece to back of mounting board and glue in place. For ornament back, repeat with backing fabric and remaining mounting board.

Beginning and ending at bottom point of stitched piece, glue cording seam allowance to wrong side of ornament front, overlapping ends of cording. For hanger, fold cord in half. Referring to photo, glue to wrong side of ornament front at top point.

Matching wrong sides, glue ornament front and back together. Referring to photo, tack tassel to bottom point of ornament.

Designs by Emie Bishop.

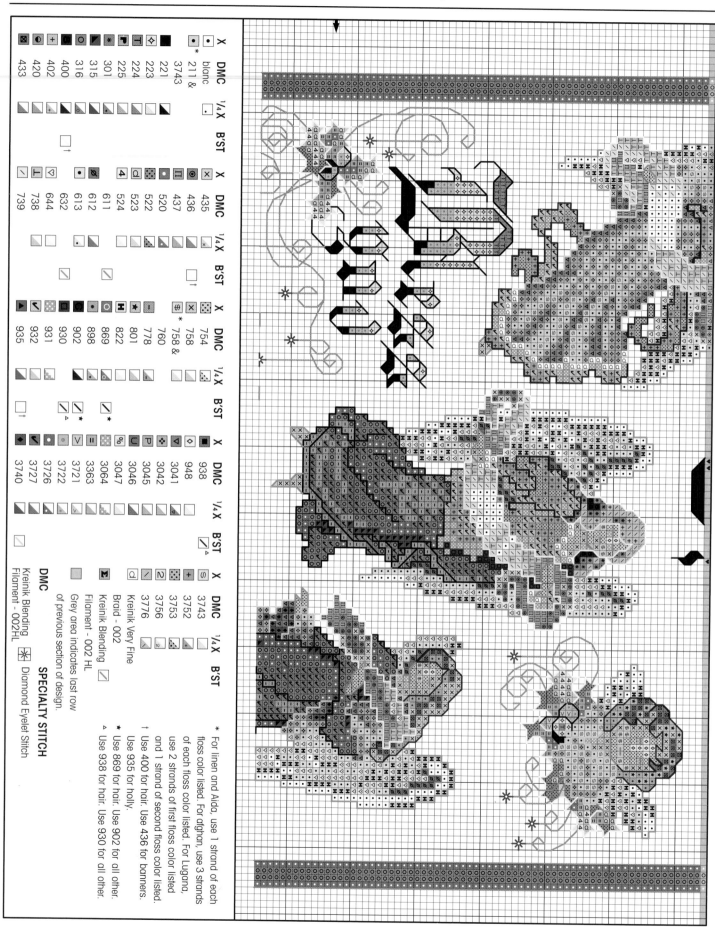

X	¼X	B'ST	DMC
	•		blanc
			211 &
			3743
			221
			223
			224
			225
			301
			315
			316
			400
			402
			420
			433

X	¼X	B'ST	DMC
			435
		†	436
			437
			520
			522
			523
			524
			611
			612
			613
			632
			644
			738
			739

X	¼X	B'ST	DMC
			754
		†	758
			758 &
			760
			778
			801
			822
		★	869
		*	898
		*	902
			930
			931
			932
		†	935

X	¼X	B'ST	DMC
		△	938
			948
			3041
			3042
			3045
			3046
			3047
			3064
			3363
			3721
			3722
			3726
			3727
			3740

X	DMC
	3743
	3752
	3753
	3756
	3776

DMC
Kreinik Very Fine Braid - 002
Kreinik Blending Filament - 002 HL
Kreinik Blending Filament - 002HL

Grey area indicates last row of previous section of design.

SPECIALTY STITCH
Diamond Eyelet Stitch

* For linen and Aida, use 1 strand of each floss color listed. For afghan, use 3 strands of each floss color listed. For Lugano, use 2 strands of first floss color listed and 1 strand of second floss color listed.
† Use 400 for hair. Use 436 for banners.
‡ Use 935 for holly.
★ Use 869 for hair. Use 902 for all other.
△ Use 938 for hair. Use 930 for all other.

CHRISTMAS BLESSINGS

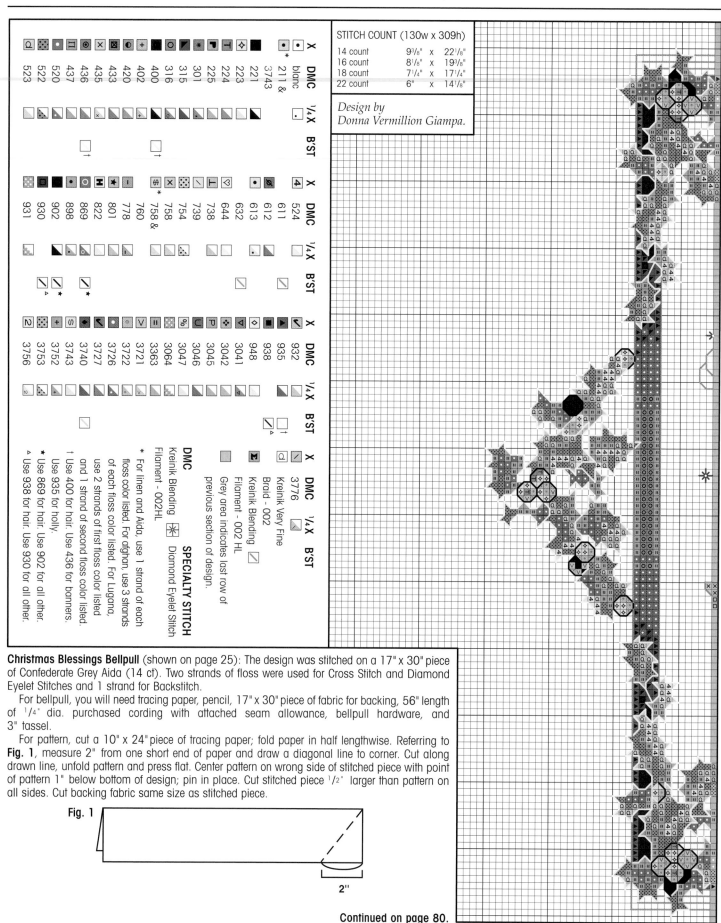

STITCH COUNT (130w x 309h)	
14 count	9 3/8" x 22 1/8"
16 count	8 1/8" x 19 3/8"
18 count	7 1/4" x 17 1/4"
22 count	6" x 14 1/8"

Design by Donna Vermillion Giampa.

DMC color key (X · ¼X · B'ST · DMC):

523, 522, 520, 437, 436, 435, 433, 420, 402, 400, 316, 315, 301, 225, 224, 223, 221, 3743, 211 &, blanc

524, 611, 612, 613, 632, 644, 738, 739, 754, 758, 758 &, 760, 778, 801, 822, 869, 898, 902, 930, 931

932, 935, 938, 948, 3041, 3042, 3045, 3046, 3047, 3064, 3363, 3721, 3722, 3726, 3727, 3740, 3743, 3752, 3753, 3756

3776

* For linen and Aida, use 1 strand of each floss color listed. For afghan, use 3 strands of each floss color listed. For Lugana, use 2 strands of each floss color listed and 1 strand of second floss color listed.

† Use 400 for hair. Use 436 for banners.

† Use 935 for holly.

★ Use 869 for hair. Use 902 for all other.

▲ Use 938 for hair. Use 930 for all other.

DMC
Kreinik Blending Filament - 002HL
Kreinik Very Fine Braid - 002
Kreinik Blending Filament - 002 HL
Grey area indicates last row of previous section of design.

SPECIALTY STITCH
Diamond Eyelet Stitch

Christmas Blessings Bellpull (shown on page 25): The design was stitched on a 17" x 30" piece of Confederate Grey Aida (14 ct). Two strands of floss were used for Cross Stitch and Diamond Eyelet Stitches and 1 strand for Backstitch.

For bellpull, you will need tracing paper, pencil, 17" x 30" piece of fabric for backing, 56" length of 1/4" dia. purchased cording with attached seam allowance, bellpull hardware, and 3" tassel.

For pattern, cut a 10" x 24" piece of tracing paper; fold paper in half lengthwise. Referring to **Fig. 1**, measure 2" from one short end of paper and draw a diagonal line to corner. Cut along drawn line, unfold pattern and press flat. Center pattern on wrong side of stitched piece with point of pattern 1" below bottom of design; pin in place. Cut stitched piece 1/2" larger than pattern on all sides. Cut backing fabric same size as stitched piece.

Fig. 1

2"

Continued on page 80.

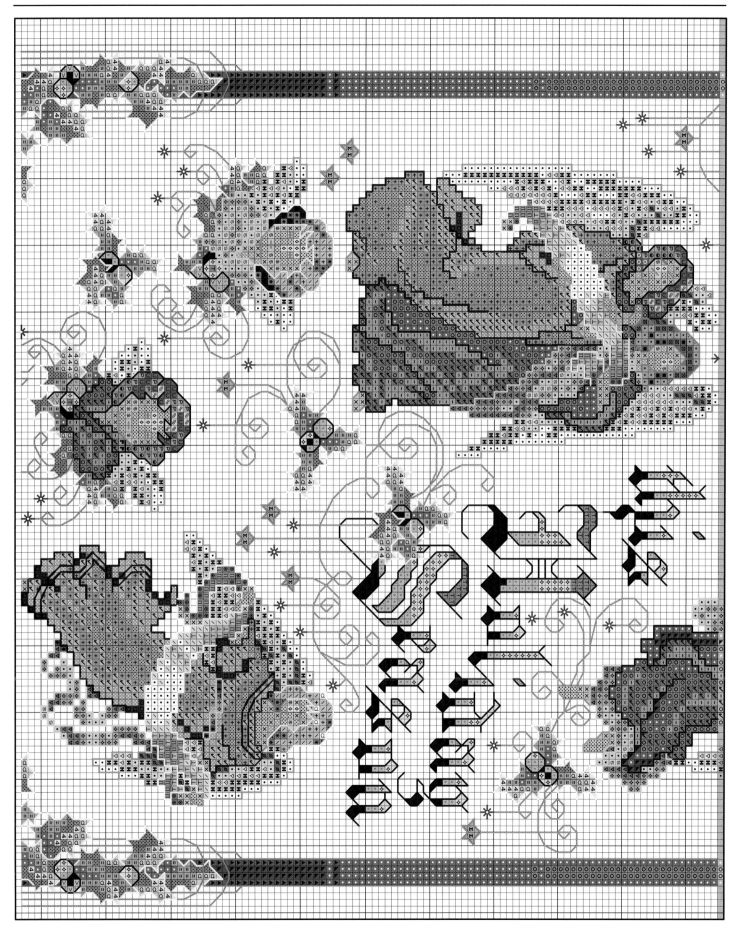

CHRISTMAS BLESSINGS

If needed, trim seam allowance of cording to ¹/₂". Matching raw edges and beginning at one top corner of stitched piece, baste cording to right side of stitched piece. Make ³/₈" clips in seam allowance of cording at corners.

Matching right sides and raw edges and leaving top edge open, use a ¹/₂" seam allowance to sew backing fabric to stitched piece. Trim corners diagonally; turn stitched piece right side out, carefully pushing corners outward. Press top edge ¹/₂" to back of bellpull. Fold top edge 1" to back; whipstitch pressed edge to back of bellpull and insert bellpull hardware. Referring to photo, tack tassel to bottom point of bellpull.

Christmas Angel in Frame (shown on page 22): A portion of the design (refer to photo) was stitched over 2 fabric threads on a 12" square of Zweigart® Cream Cashel Linen® (28 ct). Two strands of floss were used for Cross Stitch and 1 strand for Backstitch. It was custom framed.

Angel Afghan (shown on page 23): Portions of the design (refer to photo) were stitched over 2 fabric threads on a 45" x 58" piece of Ivory All-Cotton Anne Cloth (18 ct).

For afghan, cut selvages from fabric; measure 5¹/₂" from raw edge of fabric and pull out one fabric thread. Fringe fabric up to missing fabric thread. Repeat for each side. Tie an overhand knot at each corner with 4 horizontal and 4 vertical fabric threads. Working from corners, use 8 fabric threads for each knot until all threads are knotted.

Refer to Diagram for placement of designs on afghan; use 6 strands of floss for Cross Stitch and 2 strands for Backstitch.

DIAGRAM

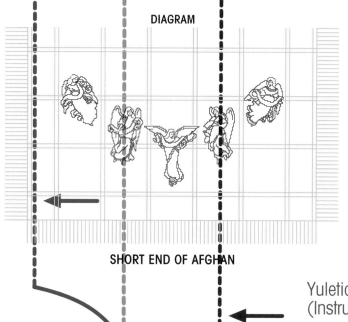

SHORT END OF AFGHAN

Angel Ornaments (shown on page 24): Portions of the design (refer to photo) were each stitched over 2 fabric threads on a 6" square of Zweigart® Ivory Lugana (25 ct). Three strands of floss were used for Cross Stitch and 1 strand for Backstitch.

For each ornament, you will need a 4" dia. circle of Ivory Lugana for backing, two 3" dia. circles of adhesive mounting board, two 3" dia. circles of batting, 12" length of ¹/₄" dia. purchased cording with attached seam allowance, and clear-drying craft glue.

Centering design, trim stitched piece to a 4" dia. circle.

Remove paper from one piece of mounting board and press one batting piece onto mounting board. Repeat with remaining mounting board and batting piece.

Clip ³/₈" into edge of stitched piece at ¹/₂" intervals. Center stitched piece over batting on one mounting board piece; fold edges of stitched piece to back of mounting board and glue in place. For ornament back, repeat with backing fabric and remaining mounting board.

Beginning and ending at top center of stitched piece, glue cording seam allowance to wrong side of ornament front, overlapping ends of cording. Matching wrong sides, glue ornament front and back together.

"Bless You" Hanging Pillow (shown on page 24): A portion of the design (refer to photo) was stitched over 2 fabric threads on a 9" square of Zweigart® Ivory Lugana (25 ct). Three strands of floss were used for Cross Stitch and 1 strand for Backstitch.

For pillow, you will need a 6" x 5¹/₄" piece of fabric for pillow backing, 22" length of ¹/₄" dia. purchased cording with attached seam allowance, an 11" length of ¹/₈" dia. satin cord for hanger, 3" tassel, and polyester fiberfill.

Centering design, trim stitched piece to measure 6" x 5¹/₄".

If needed, trim seam allowance of cording to ¹/₂"; pin cording to right side of stitched piece, making a ³/₈" clip in seam allowance of cording at corners. Ends of cording should overlap approximately 4". Turn overlapped ends of cording toward outside edge of stitched piece; baste cording to stitched piece.

Matching right sides and raw edges, pin stitched piece and backing fabric together. Leaving an opening for turning, use a ¹/₂" seam allowance to sew pillow front and backing fabric together. Trim seam allowances diagonally at corners; turn pillow right side out, carefully pushing corners outward. Stuff pillow with polyester fiberfill and blind stitch opening closed.

For hanger, refer to photo and tack ends of satin cord to each upper corner of pillow back. Referring to photo, tack tassel to bottom center of pillow.

Yuletide Toys Stocking Pattern
(Instructions on pages 70-71.)

STOCKING TOP

STOCKING MIDDLE

STOCKING BOTTOM

FROSTY FUN

Snowflake Border Scarf (shown on page 38): The design was stitched over an 11" x 5" piece of 11 mesh waste canvas across one short end of a purchased scarf with bottom of design 1" from short edge. Referring to photo, repeat top and bottom borders to each side. Three strands of floss were used for Cross Stitch. See Working on Waste Canvas, page 95.

Snowflake Gloves (shown on page 38): The small snowflake design was stitched over a 3" x 4" piece of 12 mesh waste canvas on a pair of purchased gloves. Refer to photo for placement of design. Three strands of floss were used for Cross Stitch. See Working on Waste Canvas, page 95.

Design by Deborah Lambein.

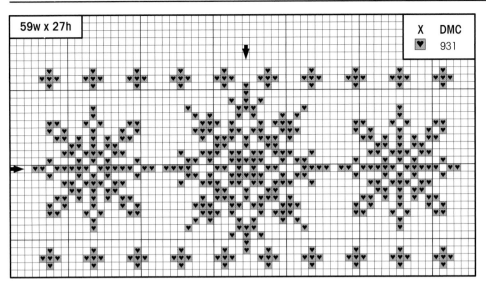

59w x 27h

X	DMC
♥	931

FINISHING INSTRUCTIONS

Father Winter Afghan (shown on page 18, chart on pages 56-59).

For afghan, you will need approximately 5½" yds of 3¼" long purchased fringe.

Cut 1½" from all edges of afghan fabric. Turn raw edges of afghan ½" to wrong side and press; turn ½" to wrong side again and baste. Referring to photo, pin straight edge of fringe to wrong side of afghan. Machine stitch around edges of afghan through all layers.

DIAGRAM

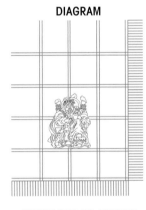

SHORT END OF AFGHAN

Woodland Border Ornaments (shown on page 16, chart on pages 58-59).

Centering design, trim stitched piece to measure 3½" square.

For each ornament, you will need a 3½" square piece of Moss Green Lugana for backing, two 1⅝" square pieces of adhesive mounting board, two 1⅝" square pieces of batting, 5" length of ⅛" dia. satin cord for hanger, 1½" tassel, and clear-drying craft glue.

Remove paper from one piece of mounting board and press one batting piece onto mounting board. Repeat with remaining mounting board and batting. Center wrong side of stitched piece over batting on one mounting board piece; fold edges of stitched piece to back of mounting board and glue in place. For ornament back, repeat with backing fabric and remaining mounting board.

For hanger, fold satin cord in half; referring to photo, glue ends to wrong side of ornament front. Referring to photo, glue tassel to wrong side of ornament front. Matching wrong sides, glue ornament front and back together.

Santa's Gift Bag Pattern
(Instructions on pages 46 and 48.)

FROSTY FUN

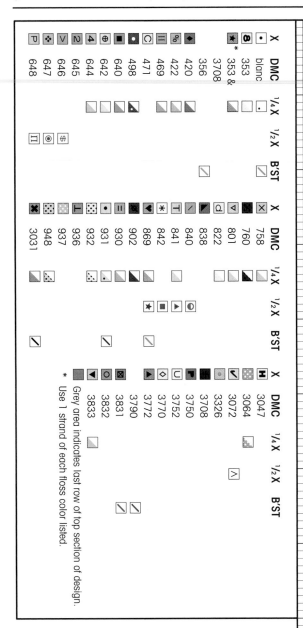

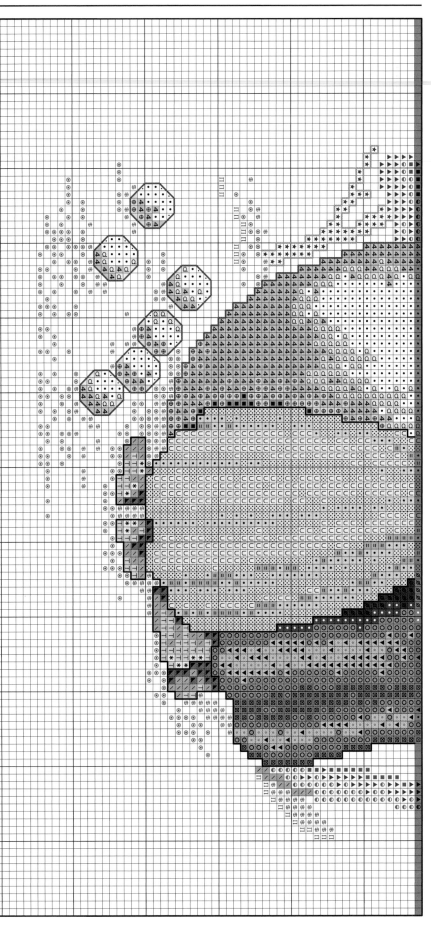

Frosty Fun in Frame (shown on page 39): The design was stitched over 2 fabric threads on a 15" x 18" piece of Zweigart® Raw Cashel Linen® (28 ct). Two strands of floss were used for Cross Stitch and 1 strand for Half Cross Stitch and Backstitch. It was custom framed.

Needlework adaptation by Carol Emmer.

STITCH COUNT (95w x 144h)

14 count	6⁷⁄₈"	x	10³⁄₈"	
16 count	6"	x	9"	
18 count	5³⁄₈"	x	8"	
22 count	4³⁄₈"	x	6⁵⁄₈"	

GLORIOUS SAMPLING

All project information on page 87.

STITCH COUNT (137w x 225h)		
14 count	9⁷⁄₈" x	16¹⁄₈"
16 count	8⁵⁄₈" x	14¹⁄₈"
18 count	7⁵⁄₈" x	12¹⁄₂"
22 count	6¹⁄₄" x	10¹⁄₄"

GLORIOUS SAMPLING

STITCH COUNT (101w x 102h)

14 count	7¼"	x	7⅜"
16 count	6⅜"	x	6⅜"
18 count	5⅝"	x	5¾"
22 count	4⅝"	x	4¾"

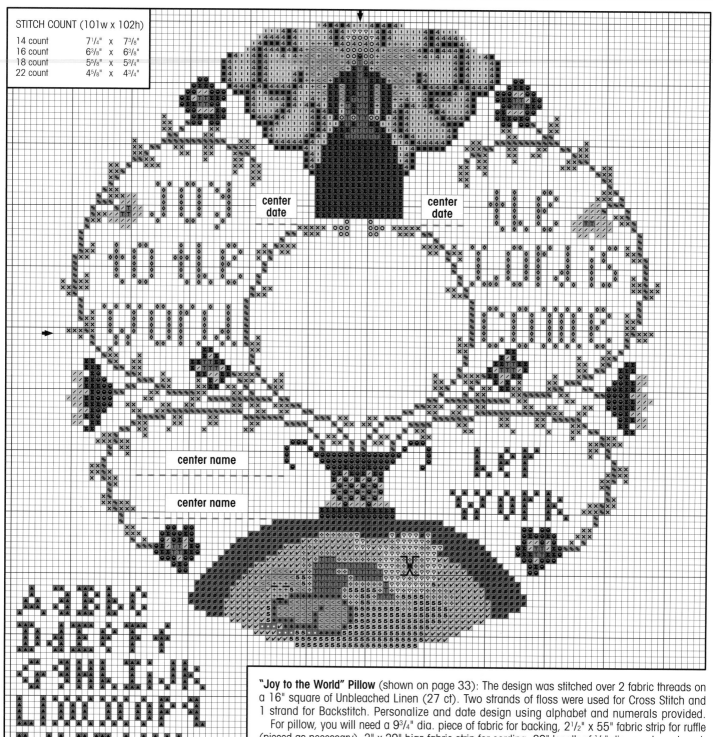

center date

center date

center name

center name

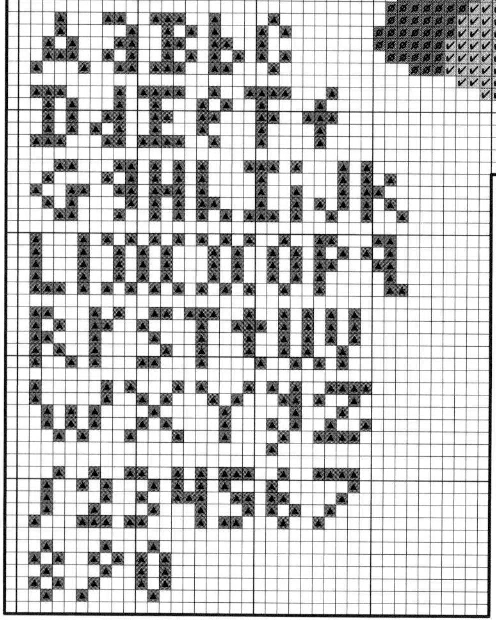

"Joy to the World" Pillow (shown on page 33): The design was stitched over 2 fabric threads on a 16" square of Unbleached Linen (27 ct). Two strands of floss were used for Cross Stitch and 1 strand for Backstitch. Personalize and date design using alphabet and numerals provided.

For pillow, you will need a 9¾" dia. piece of fabric for backing, 2½" x 55" fabric strip for ruffle (pieced as necessary), 2" x 29" bias fabric strip for cording, 29" length of ¼" dia. purchased cord, 3" x 9" fabric strip for hanger, 3" x 10" fabric strip for bow, two ⅞" dia. ready-to-cover buttons, 2 fabric pieces for buttons, and polyester fiberfill.

Centering design, trim stitched piece to measure 9¾" dia. circle.

For cording, center cord on wrong side of bias strip; matching long edges, fold strip over cord. Use a zipper foot to baste along length of strip close to cord; trim seam allowance to ½". Clip ⅜" into seam allowance of cording at ½" intervals. Matching raw edges, pin cording to right side of stitched piece. Ends of cording should overlap approximately 2"; pin overlapping end out of the way. Starting 2" from beginning end of cording and ending 4" from overlapping end, baste cording to stitched piece. On overlapping end of cording, remove 2½" of basting; fold end of fabric back and trim cord so that it meets beginning end of cord. Fold end of fabric ½" to wrong side; wrap fabric over beginning end of cording. Finish basting cording to stitched piece.

STITCH COUNT (67w x 67h)

14 count	4⁷/₈"	x	4⁷/₈"
16 count	4¹/₄"	x	4¹/₄"
18 count	3³/₄"	x	3³/₄"
22 count	3¹/₈"	x	3¹/₈"

X	DMC	B'ST	X	DMC	X	DMC	B'ST
△	318		♡	680	•	844	✓
◕	355	✓	∅	730	■	924	
✕	356		⋰	731	4	926	
◇	370		✔	732	!	927	
╱	407	✓	5	733	‰	935	
+	414		<	762	✕	937	
✳	415		❖	780	–	950	
O	422		T	781	H	3031	✓
★	632		▲	829	$	3047	

"Peace on Earth" Ornament (shown on page 32): The design was stitched over 2 fabric threads on a 9" square of Unbleached Linen (27 ct). Two strands of floss were used for Cross Stitch and 1 strand for Backstitch.

For ornament, you will need a 9" square of fabric for backing, polyester fiberfill, 15" length of twisted cord for edges, 8" length of twisted cord for hanger, and a 1¹/₄" tassel.

Matching right sides and raw edges, pin stitched piece and backing fabric together. Referring to photo, trim backing fabric and stitched piece **1" larger** than design on all sides. Leaving an opening for turning, use a ¹/₂" seam allowance to sew pieces together; trim seam allowance diagonally at corners. Turn ornament right side out, carefully pushing corners outward. Stuff ornament with polyester fiberfill; blind stitch opening closed. Blind stitch cord around edges of ornament.

For hanger, fold cord in half and tie an overhand knot ¹/₂" from ends. Referring to photo, sew hanger to top point of ornament and tassel to bottom point of ornament.

For ruffle, press short edges of fabric strip ¹/₂" to wrong side. Matching wrong sides and long edges, fold strip in half; press. Machine baste ¹/₂" from raw edges; gather fabric strip to fit stitched piece. Matching raw edges, pin ruffle to right side of stitched piece, overlapping short ends ¹/₄". Use a ¹/₂" seam allowance to sew ruffle to stitched piece.

Matching right sides and leaving an opening for turning, use a ¹/₂" seam allowance to sew stitched piece and backing fabric together. Clip seam allowances; turn pillow right side out. Stuff pillow with polyester fiberfill and blind stitch opening closed.

For buttons, follow manufacturer's instructions to cover buttons with matching fabric. Referring to photo for placement, sew buttons to front and back of pillow.

For hanger, match right sides and raw edges of fabric strip. Using ¹/₂" seam allowance, sew long edges together; turn right side out and press. Repeat for bow fabric strip. Fold hanger in half and referring to photo, sew ends to top of pillow. Tie remaining fabric strip into a bow and referring to photo, blind stitch to top of hanger.

Sampler Stocking (shown on pages 34-35, chart on pages 84-85): The design was stitched over 2 fabric threads on a 19" x 26" piece of Zweigart® Cream Dublin Linen (25 ct). Two strands of floss were used for Cross Stitch and 1 strand for Backstitch. Personalize stocking using DMC 407 floss and alphabet provided.

For stocking, you will need a 19" x 26" piece of fabric for backing, two 19" x 26" pieces of fabric for lining, 51" length of ¹/₄" dia. purchased cording

with attached seam allowance for sides and bottom edges, 18" length of ¹/₄" dia. purchased cording with attached seam allowance for top edge, and 2" x 6" piece of fabric for hanger.

Matching wrong sides and raw edges, pin stitched piece and backing fabric together. Referring to photo, trim backing fabric and stitched piece **¹/₂" larger** than design on all sides. Using stitched piece as a pattern, cut **two** from lining fabric.

If needed, trim seam allowance of cording to ¹/₂". Matching raw edges, baste cording to right side of stocking front at side and bottom edges.

Matching right sides and leaving top edge open, use a ¹/₂" seam allowance to sew stitched piece and backing fabric together. Clip seam allowance at curves and turn stocking right side out.

Beginning at center back and matching raw edges, use a ¹/₂" seam allowance to sew cording to top edge of stocking, overlapping ends of cording.

Matching right sides and leaving top edge open, use a ⁵/₈" seam allowance to sew lining pieces together; trim seam allowance close to stitching. **Do not turn lining right side out.** Press top edge of lining ¹/₂" to wrong side.

For hanger, press each long edge of fabric strip ¹/₂" to center. Matching long edges, fold strip in half and sew close to folded edges. Matching short edges, fold hanger in half and whipstitch to inside of stocking at right seam.

With wrong sides facing, place lining inside stocking; blind stitch lining to stocking.

Designs by Mary Beale.

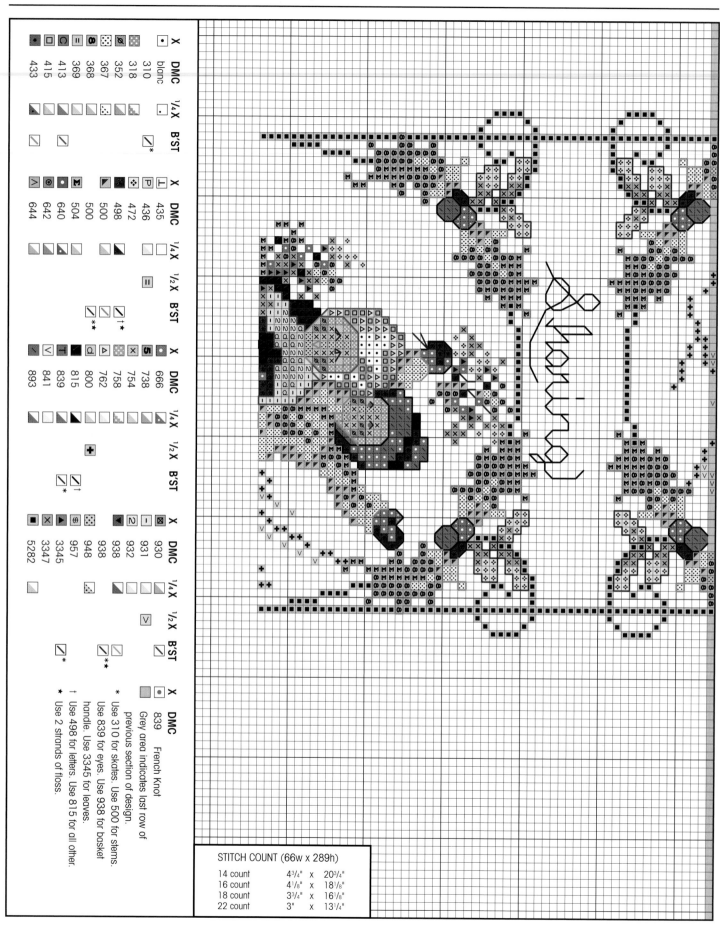

X	DMC	1/4X	B'ST
•	blanc	•	
	310		*
	318		
	352		
	367		
	368		
	369		
	413		
	415		
	433		

X	DMC	1/4X	1/2X	B'ST
	435			
P	436			*
	472			**
	498			
	500		II	
	504			
	640			
	642			
	644			

X	DMC	1/4X	1/2X	B'ST
	666			
	738			
	754			
	758			
	762		+	
5	800			t
	815			*
	839			
	841			
	893			

X	DMC	1/4X	1/2X	B'ST
	930			
	931			
2	932			
	938			
	938			
	948			
	957			**
	3345		V	*
	3347			
	5282			

X	DMC
•	839 French Knot

Grey area indicates last row of previous section of design.

* Use 310 for skates. Use 500 for stems. Use 839 for eyes. Use 938 for basket handle. Use 3345 for leaves.

† Use 498 for letters. Use 815 for all other.

★ Use 2 strands of floss.

STITCH COUNT (66w x 289h)

14 count	4 3/4"	x	20 3/4"
16 count	4 1/8"	x	18 1/8"
18 count	3 3/4"	x	16 1/8"
22 count	3"	x	13 1/4"

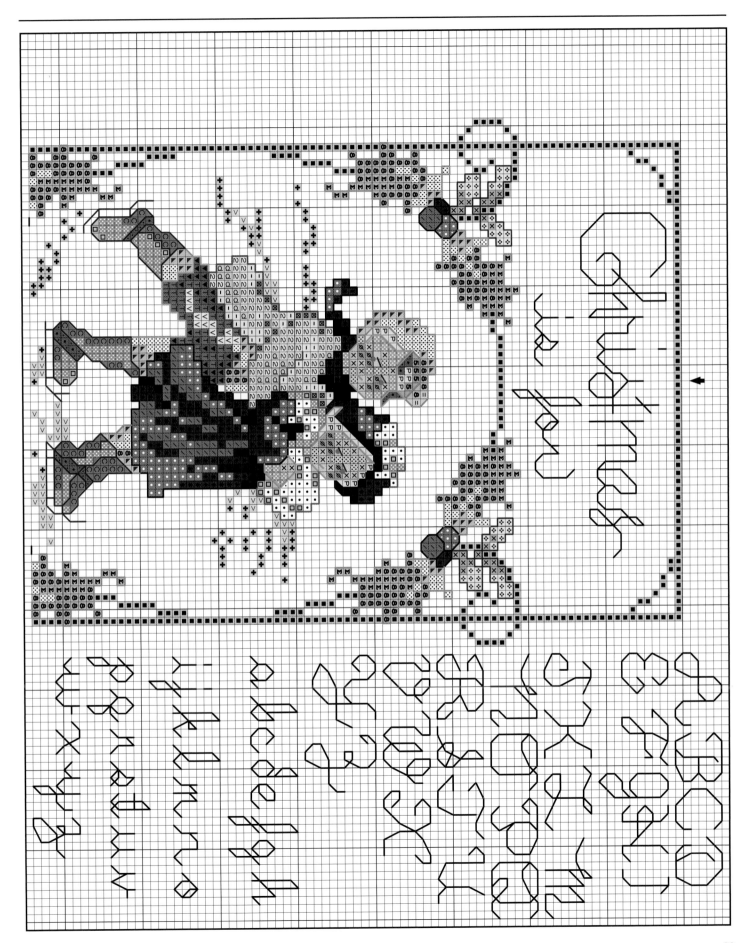

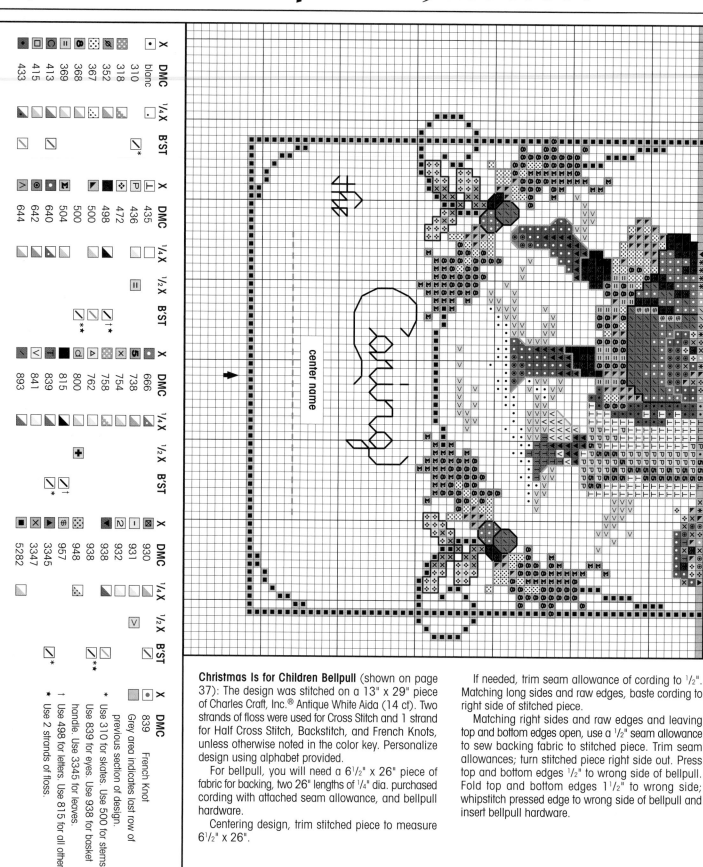

center name

X	DMC	¼X	B'ST
•	blanc		
	310		*
	318		
	352		
	367		
	368		
	369		
	413		
	415		
	433		

X	DMC	¼X	½X	B'ST
	435			
	436			
	472			
	498		II	
	500			*†
	500			**†
	504			
	640			
	642			
	644			

X	DMC	¼X	½X	B'ST
	666			
	738			
	754			**†
	758			
	762			+
	800			
	815			
	839			
	841			
	893			

X	DMC	¼X	½X	B'ST
	930			
	931			
	932			
	938			
	938			**†
	948			
	957			
	3345		V	
	3347			
	5282			*

X	DMC
•	839 French Knot
	Grey area indicates last row of previous section of design.

* Use 310 for skates. Use 500 for stems.
Use 839 for eyes. Use 938 for basket
handle. Use 3345 for leaves.

† Use 498 for letters. Use 815 for all other.

★ Use 2 strands of floss.

Christmas Is for Children Bellpull (shown on page 37): The design was stitched on a 13" x 29" piece of Charles Craft, Inc.® Antique White Aida (14 ct). Two strands of floss were used for Cross Stitch and 1 strand for Half Cross Stitch, Backstitch, and French Knots, unless otherwise noted in the color key. Personalize design using alphabet provided.

For bellpull, you will need a 6½" x 26" piece of fabric for backing, two 26" lengths of ¼" dia. purchased cording with attached seam allowance, and bellpull hardware.

Centering design, trim stitched piece to measure 6½" x 26".

If needed, trim seam allowance of cording to ½". Matching long sides and raw edges, baste cording to right side of stitched piece.

Matching right sides and raw edges and leaving top and bottom edges open, use a ½" seam allowance to sew backing fabric to stitched piece. Trim seam allowances; turn stitched piece right side out. Press top and bottom edges ½" to wrong side of bellpull. Fold top and bottom edges 1½" to wrong side; whipstitch pressed edge to wrong side of bellpull and insert bellpull hardware.

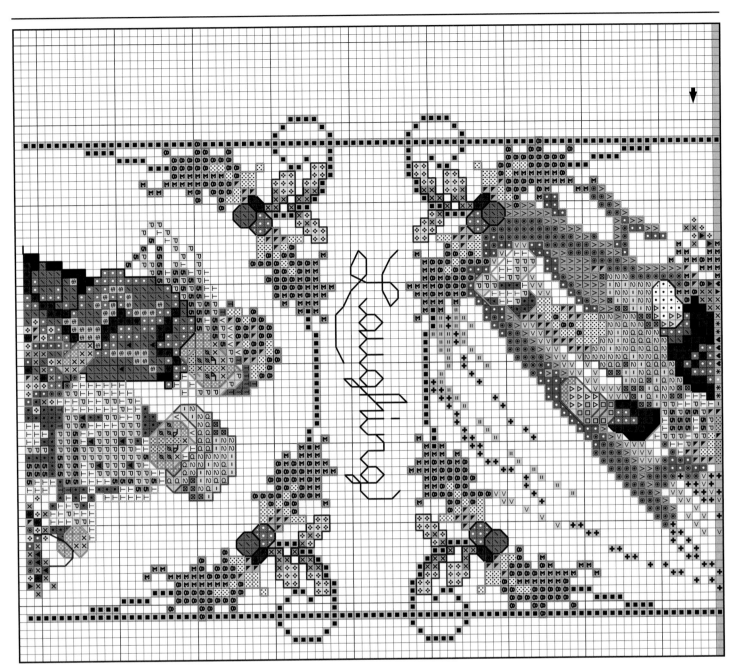

Winter Fun Pillow (shown on page 36): A portion of the design (refer to photo) was stitched on a 13" square of Charles Craft, Inc.® Antique White Aida (14 ct). Two strands of floss were used for Cross Stitch and 1 strand for Half Cross Stitch, Backstitch, and French Knots.

For pillow, you will need an 11³/₄" x 12¹/₂" piece of fabric for backing, two 6¹/₄" x 3³/₄" strips of fabric for top and bottom borders, two 3³/₄" x 12¹/₂" strips of fabric for side borders, 49" length of ¹/₄" dia. purchased cording with attached seam allowance, and polyester fiberfill.

Centering design, trim stitched piece to measure 6¹/₄" x 7".

Note: When piecing pillow, always match right sides and raw edges. Use a ¹/₂" seam allowance for all seams.

For pillow front, sew top border strip to top edge of stitched piece. Repeat with bottom border strip and bottom edge. Press seam allowances toward strips. Sew one side border strip to one side edge of stitched piece and top

and bottom strips. Repeat with remaining side border strip and side edge.

If needed, trim seam allowance of cording to ¹/₂"; pin cording to right side of pillow front making a ³/₈" clip in seam allowance of cording at corners. Ends of cording should overlap approximately 4". Turn overlapped ends of cording toward outside edge of pillow front; baste cording to pillow front.

Matching right sides and raw edges and leaving an opening for turning, sew pillow front and backing fabric together. Trim seam allowances diagonally at corners; turn pillow right side out, carefully pushing corners outward. Stuff pillow with polyester fiberfill and blind stitch opening closed.

Design by Donna Vermillion Giampa.

TINY TREASURES

Playing in the Snow in Frame (shown on page 41)

X	DMC	¼ X	½ X	B'ST
•	blanc	•	❖	
◗	326	◪		
◼	335	◪		
◕	353			
★*	353 &			
	3708			
	356		◪	
♥	433	◪	◪ †	
⊠	435	◪	◪	
✚*	469			
= *	470			
	610		◪ †	
▬	640	◪	◪	
⊕	642	◪		
4	644	◻		
⁄⁄	676		V	
H	677		◆	
$	680	◪	◒	
5	729		%	
✕	758			
◼	815	◪	◪ ▲	
∧	818			
✔	822	◻		
◉	899			
⊥	926		U	
◣	927		▽	
C	928	◻		
▦	932			
▦	948	◹		
	3031		◪	
▦	3064			
Π	3326			
◼	3708			
Σ	3712	◪	◪ ▲	
	3768		◪ ▲	
◇	3770	◻		
▲	3772	◪		

* Use 1 strand of each floss color listed.
† Use 610 for sweater. Use 433 for all other.
★ Use 1 strand of floss.
▲ Use 815 for scarf. Use 3712 for lips. Use 3768 for snowballs.

58w x 81h

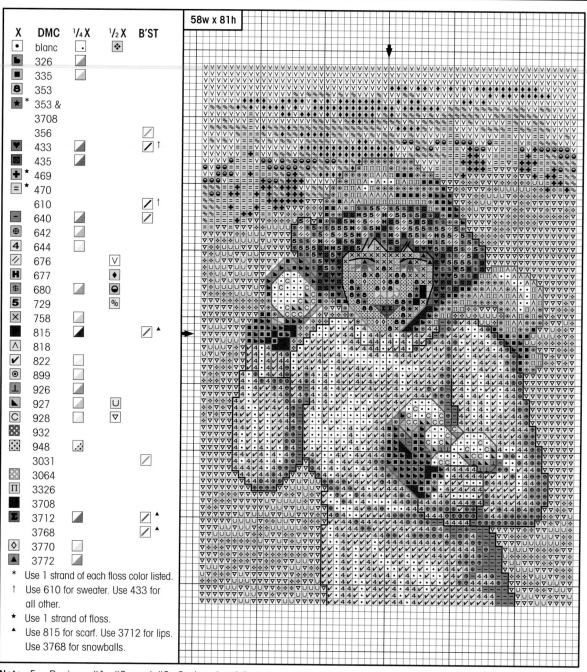

Playing in the Snow in Frame (shown on page 41): The design was stitched over 2 fabric threads on a 12" x 14" piece of Zweigart® Cream Cashel Linen® (28 ct). Two strands of floss were used for Cross Stitch and 1 strand for Half Cross Stitch and Backstitch, unless otherwise noted in the color key. It was inserted in a purchased frame (5" x 7" opening).

For frame, you will need assorted buttons and charms, gold paint, and clear-drying craft glue. Referring to photo, glue assorted buttons and charms to frame. Spray buttons, charms, and frame with gold paint; let dry.

Needlework adaptation by Carol Emmer.

Note: For Designs #1, #2, and #3, 2 strands of floss were used for Cross Stitch and 1 strand for Backstitch. Attach beads using 1 strand of DMC 822 floss for gold beads and 1 strand of DMC 3328 floss for red beads. See Attaching Beads, page 95. Refer to chart for number of strands used for Specialty Stitches. See Specialty Stitch Diagrams, page 96.

Poinsettia Purse Ornament (shown on page 40): Design #1 was stitched over 2 fabric threads on a 6" square of Zweigart® Cream Cashel Linen® (28ct).

For purse ornament, you will need a 2½" purse clasp, a 6" square of Cream Cashel Linen® for backing, tracing paper, fabric marking pencil, and two 15" lengths of ⅛"w ribbon for hanger.

For pattern, fold tracing paper in half and place fold on dashed line of pattern; trace pattern onto tracing paper. Cut out pattern; unfold and press flat. Referring to photo, position pattern on wrong side of stitched piece; pin pattern in place. Use fabric marking pencil to draw around pattern; remove pattern. Matching right sides and raw edges, pin stitched piece and backing fabric together.

Leaving top and upper side edges open (pink line on pattern), sew directly on drawn line; remove pins. Trim top edges ½" from drawn line and trim seam allowances to ½"; clip curves. Turn top edges ½" to wrong side and press. Turn purse ornament right side out.

Open purse clasp and position sides of purse under side hinges of clasp and top edges of purse inside clasp. Using DMC ecru floss, attach upper edges of purse to each side of clasp.

For hanger, thread ribbons through openings on top of clasp. Referring to photo, tie ribbons in a bow. Trim ends as desired.

Holly Box (shown on page 40): Design #2 was stitched on a 5" x 6" piece of Cream perforated paper (14 ct).

For box, you will need a 4½" x 3¼" papier maché box, gold acrylic paint, sponge paintbrush, 17" length of ½"w braid, and clear-drying craft glue.

Centering design, trim stitched piece to measure 4½" x 3¼".

Paint box gold and let dry. Glue stitched piece to box lid. Referring to photo, glue braid around edge of lid.

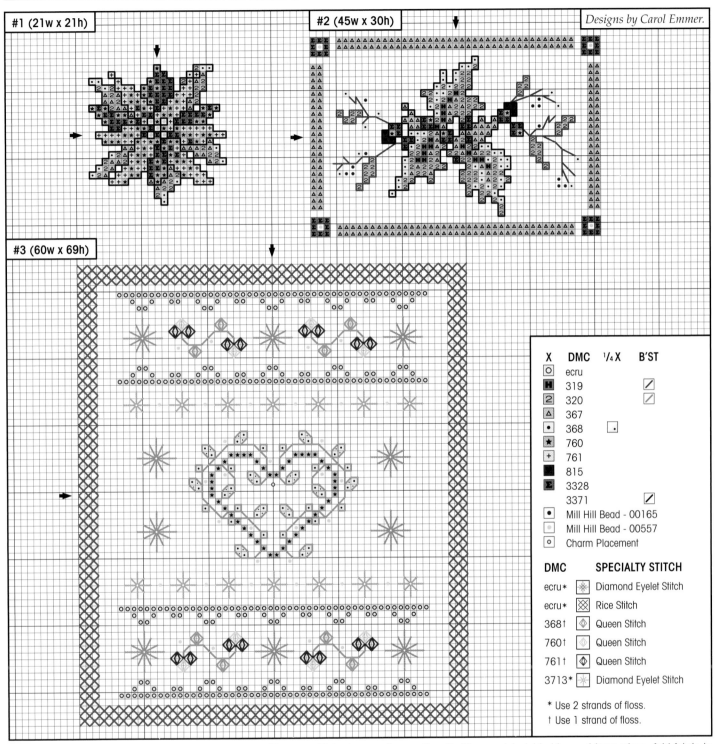

#1 (21w x 21h)

#2 (45w x 30h)

Designs by Carol Emmer.

#3 (60w x 69h)

X	DMC	¼ X	B'ST
O	ecru		
H	319		╱
2	320		╱
▲	367		
•	368	•	
★	760		
+	761		
■	815		
Σ	3328		
	3371		╱
•	Mill Hill Bead - 00165		
▣	Mill Hill Bead - 00557		
o	Charm Placement		

DMC		SPECIALTY STITCH
ecru*	✳	Diamond Eyelet Stitch
ecru*	⊠	Rice Stitch
368†	◈	Queen Stitch
760†	◈	Queen Stitch
761†	◈	Queen Stitch
3713*	✳	Diamond Eyelet Stitch

* Use 2 strands of floss.
† Use 1 strand of floss.

Heart Needle Roll (shown on page 41): Design #3 was stitched over 2 fabric threads on a 12" x 13" piece of Zweigart® Cream Cashel Linen® (28 ct).

For needle roll, you will need a 6¹⁄₂" x 11¹⁄₂" piece of fabric for needle roll pillow, two 6¹⁄₂" lengths of ³⁄₄"w flat lace, polyester fiberfill, two 14" lengths of ¹⁄₄"w ribbon, and a heart charm.

Centering design, trim stitched piece to measure 6¹⁄₂" x 9¹⁄₂".

Matching right sides and long edges, fold stitched piece in half. Using a ¹⁄₄" seam allowance, sew long edges together; trim seam allowance to ¹⁄₈" and turn stitched piece right side out. With seam centered in back, press stitched piece flat.

For needle roll pillow, match right sides and long edges; fold fabric in half. Using a ¹⁄₂" seam allowance, sew long edges together. Turn short edges ¹⁄₄" to wrong side and press; turn ¹⁄₄" to wrong side again and hem. Press short edges of lace ¹⁄₂" to wrong side. Blind stitch straight edge of lace to each short edge of pillow; turn pillow right side out. Referring to photo, stuff pillow with polyester fiberfill; tie ribbons around each end.

Wrap stitched piece around needle roll pillow, turning raw edges to wrong side so that ends meet; blind stitch short ends together.

Design by Lorrie Birmingham.

YULETIDE TOYS

Yuletide Toys Stocking (shown on page 27, chart on pages 68-71).

X	DMC	¼ X	B'ST
■	321	◢	
⊙	335		
	500		◢
▦	561	◢	
Π	562	◢	
✳	814	◢	
◉	816	◢	
	902		◢
♡	913	◢	

GENERAL INSTRUCTIONS

WORKING WITH CHARTS

How to Read Charts: Each of the designs is shown in chart form. Each colored square on the chart represents one Cross Stitch or one Half Cross Stitch. Each colored triangle on the chart represents one Quarter Stitch. In some charts, reduced symbols are used to indicate Quarter Stitches (**Fig. 1**). **Fig. 2** and **Fig. 3** indicate Cross Stitch under Backstitch.

Fig. 1   **Fig. 2** 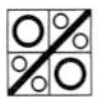   **Fig. 3**

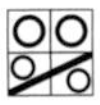

Black or colored dots on the chart represent Cross Stitch, French Knots, or bead placement. The black or colored straight lines on the chart indicate Backstitch. The symbol is omitted or reduced when a French Knot, Backstitch, or bead covers a square.

Each chart is accompanied by a color key. This key indicates the color of floss to use for each stitch on the chart. The headings on the color key are for Cross Stitch (**X**), DMC color number (**DMC**), Quarter Stitch (**¼X**), Half Cross Stitch (**½X**), and Backstitch (**B'ST**). Color key columns should be read vertically and horizontally to determine type of stitch and floss color. Some designs may include stitches worked with metallic thread, such as blending filament or braid. The metallic thread may be blended with floss or used alone. If any metallic thread is used in a design, the color key will contain the necessary information.

STITCHING TIPS

Attaching Beads: Refer to chart for bead placement and sew bead in place using a fine needle that will pass through bead. Bring needle up at 1, run needle through bead and then down at 2. Secure floss on back or move to next bead as shown in **Fig. 4**.

Fig. 4

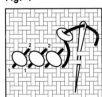

Working on Waste Canvas: Waste canvas is a special canvas that provides an evenweave grid for placing stitches on fabric. After the design is worked over the canvas, the canvas threads are removed, leaving the design on the fabric. The canvas is available in several mesh sizes.

Cover edges of canvas with masking tape. Cut a piece of lightweight non-fusible interfacing the same size as canvas to provide a firm stitching base.

Find desired stitching area and mark center of area with a pin. Match center of canvas to pin.

Use the blue threads in canvas to place canvas straight on garment; pin canvas to garment. Pin interfacing to wrong side of garment. Baste all layers together as shown in **Fig. 5**.

Using a sharp needle, work design, stitching from large holes to large holes. Trim canvas to within ¾" of design. Dampen canvas until it becomes limp. Pull out canvas threads one at a time using tweezers (**Fig. 6**). Trim interfacing close to design.

Fig. 5   **Fig. 6**

STITCH DIAGRAMS

Note: Bring threaded needle up at 1 and all odd numbers and down at 2 and all even numbers.

Counted Cross Stitch (X): Work one Cross Stitch to correspond to each colored square on the chart. For horizontal rows, work stitches in two journeys (**Fig. 7**). For vertical rows, complete each stitch as shown (**Fig. 8**). When working over two fabric threads, work Cross Stitch as shown in **Fig. 9**. When the chart shows a Backstitch crossing a colored square (**Fig. 10**), a Cross Stitch should be worked first; then the Backstitch (**Fig. 15** or **16**) should be worked on top of the Cross Stitch.

Fig. 7   **Fig. 8**

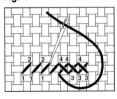

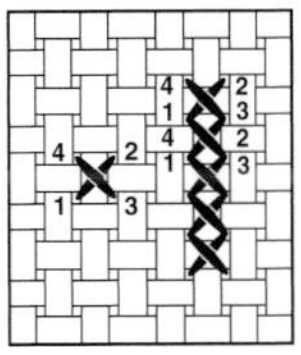

Fig. 9 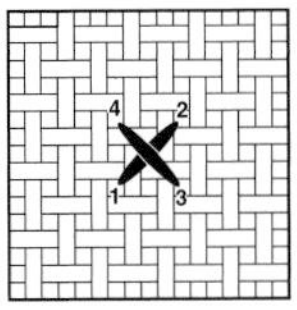   **Fig. 10**

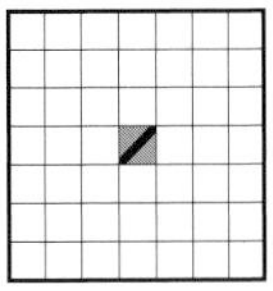

Quarter Stitch (¼X): Quarter Stitches are denoted by triangular shapes of color on the chart and on the color key. For a Quarter Stitch, come up at 1 (**Fig. 11**), then split fabric thread to go down at 2. **Fig. 12** shows the technique for Quarter Stitches when working over two fabric threads.

Fig. 11   **Fig. 12**

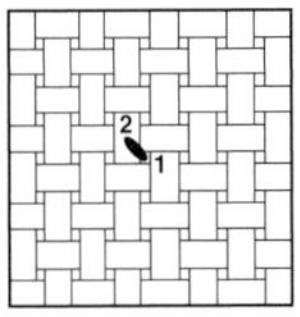

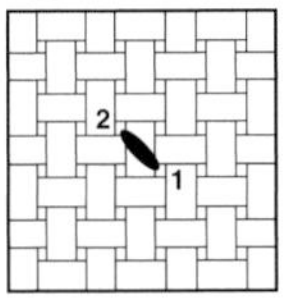

Half Cross Stitch (½X): This stitch is one journey of the Cross Stitch and is worked from lower left to upper right as shown in **Fig. 13**. When working over two fabric threads, work Half Cross Stitch as shown in **Fig. 14**.

Fig. 13   **Fig. 14**

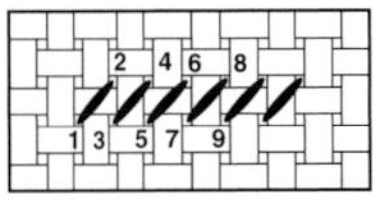

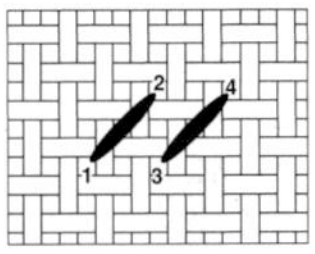

Backstitch (B'ST): For outline detail, Backstitch (shown on chart and on color key by black or colored straight lines) should be worked after the design has been completed (**Fig. 15**). When working over two fabric threads, work Backstitch as shown in **Fig. 16**.

Fig. 15   **Fig. 16**

 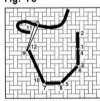

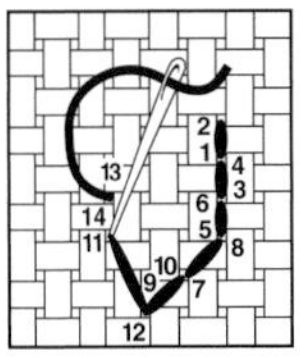

French Knot: Bring needle up at 1. Wrap floss once around needle and insert needle at 2, holding end of floss with non-stitching fingers (**Fig. 17**). Tighten knot, then pull needle through fabric, holding floss until it must be released. For larger knot, use more strands of floss; wrap only once.

Fig. 17

Continued on page 96.

Lazy Daisy Stitch: Bring needle up at 1 and make a loop. Go down at 1 and come up at 2, keeping floss below point of needle (**Fig. 18**). Pull needle through and go down at 2 to anchor loop, completing stitch. (**Note:** To support stitches, it may be helpful to go down in edge of next fabric thread when anchoring loop.)

Fig. 18

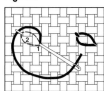

SPECIALTY STITCH DIAGRAMS

Note: Bring threaded needle up at 1 and all odd numbers and down at 2 and all even numbers.

PULLED STITCHES

When working Pulled Stitches, fabric threads should be pulled tightly together to create an opening in the fabric around the stitch. Figs. show placement of stitch but do not show pulling of the fabric threads. Keep tension even throughout work.

Algerian Eye Stitch: An "eye" is formed in the center of this stitch. Come up at 1, go down in center, and pull tightly toward 3. Come up at 3, go down in center, and pull tightly toward 5; continue working in this manner until stitch is complete (stitches 5-15) (**Fig. 19**).

Fig. 19

Diamond Eyelet and **Half Diamond Eyelet Stitches:** An "eye" is formed in the center of this stitch. Come up at 1, go down in center, and pull tightly toward 3. Come up at 3, go down in center, and pull tightly toward 5; continue working in this manner until stitch is complete (stitches 5-31) as shown in **Fig. 20.** For **Half Diamond Eyelet** work stitches 1-17 in the same manner. The number of threads worked over will vary according to the chart.

Fig. 20

Four-sided Eyelet Stitch: An "eye" is formed in the center of this stitch. Come up at 1, go down in center, and pull tightly toward 3. Come up at 3, go down in center, and pull tightly toward 5; continue working in this manner until stitch is complete as shown in **Fig. 21.**

Fig. 21

EMBROIDERY STITCHES

Long Arm Cross Stitch: This overlapping stitch is worked continuously from left to right. Complete first stitch (stitches 1-4); then work next stitch (stitches 5-8) as shown in **Fig. 22.** Work all consecutive stitches in the same manner as stitches 5-8.

Fig. 22

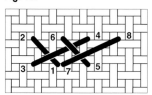

Queen Stitch: This decorative stitch forms a diamond shape. Work a long stitch (stitch 1-2) loosely and catch with a short stitch (stitch 3-4) (**Fig. 23a**). Complete stitch (stitches 5-16), catching each long stitch with a short stitch as shown in **Figs. 23a-c.**

Fig. 23a   **Fig. 23b**   **Fig. 23c**

Rice Stitch: This decorative stitch is formed by first working a large Cross Stitch (stitches 1-4) and then working a stitch over each leg of the Cross Stitch (stitches 5-12) as shown in **Fig. 24.**

Fig. 24

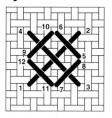

Satin Stitch: This stitch is a series of straight stitches worked side by side (**Fig. 25**). The number of threads worked over and the direction of stitches will vary according to the chart.

Fig. 25

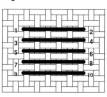

Whipped Backstitch: This stitch is formed by working a series of Backstitches (stitches 1-8) and then whipping these stitches with an alternate floss color starting at A and working towards B as shown in **Fig. 26.**

Fig. 26

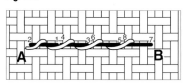

Photo models were stitched using DMC floss, courtesy of The DMC Corporation.

Instructions tested and photo items made by Debbie Anderson, Muriel Hicks, Connie Irby, Elizabeth James, Pat Johnson, Wanda J. Linsley, Patricia O'Neil, Angie Perryman, Stephanie Gail Sharp, Anne Simpson Lavonne Sims, Carolyn Smith, Helen Stanton, Trist Vines, and Sharon Woods.